Alabama

Statehood: December 14, 1819 – 22nd

Area: 51,609 square miles

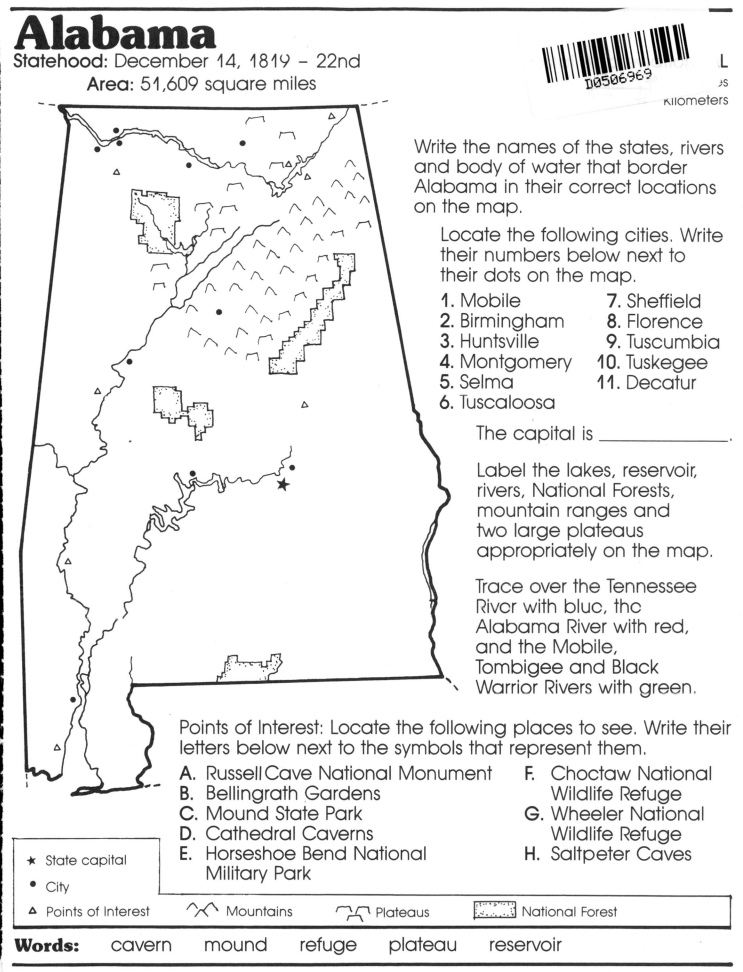

Write the names of the states, rivers and body of water that border Alabama in their correct locations on the map.

Locate the following cities. Write their numbers below next to their dots on the map.

1. Mobile
2. Birmingham
3. Huntsville
4. Montgomery
5. Selma
6. Tuscaloosa
7. Sheffield
8. Florence
9. Tuscumbia
10. Tuskegee
11. Decatur

The capital is _____.

Label the lakes, reservoir, rivers, National Forests, mountain ranges and two large plateaus appropriately on the map.

Trace over the Tennessee River with blue, the Alabama River with red, and the Mobile, Tombigee and Black Warrior Rivers with green.

Points of Interest: Locate the following places to see. Write their letters below next to the symbols that represent them.

A. Russell Cave National Monument
B. Bellingrath Gardens
C. Mound State Park
D. Cathedral Caverns
E. Horseshoe Bend National Military Park
F. Choctaw National Wildlife Refuge
G. Wheeler National Wildlife Refuge
H. Saltpeter Caves

★ State capital
● City
△ Points of Interest
⌃⌃ Mountains
Plateaus
National Forest

Words: cavern   mound   refuge   plateau   reservoir

Alaska

Statehood: January 3, 1959 – 49th
Postal Abbreviation: AK
Area: 599,757 square miles

250 Miles
250 Kilometers

* State capital
• City
△ Points of Interest
∧∧∧ Mountains
☐ National Park

Write the names of the territory, province and bodies of water that border Alaska in their correct locations on the map.

Locate the following cities. Write their numbers below next to their dots on the map.

1. Anchorage	3. Barrow	5. Nome	7. Juneau	9. Seward
2. Fairbanks	4. Kotzebue	6. Valdez	8. Ketchikan	

The capital is _____.

Label the mountain ranges, rivers, National Parks and Alexander Archipelago appropriately on the map. Circle the Aleutian Islands. Mark an **X** on Kodiak Island. Trace over the International Dateline with red. Trace over the Arctic Circle with green. Mark an **S** on Seward Peninsula.

Points of Interest: Locate the following places to see. Write their letters below next to the symbols that represent them.

A. Mount McKinley **D.** Point Barrow Naval Arctic **F.** Sitka National Historic Park
B. Anaktuvuk Pass   Research Laboratory **G.** Kenai Fiords National Park
C. Diomede Islands **E.** Trans Alaska Pipeline

Words: glacier   arctic   aleut   archipelago   peninsula   fiord   fjord

Arizona

Statehood: February 14, 1912 – 48th

Postal Abbreviation: AZ

Area: 113,909 square miles

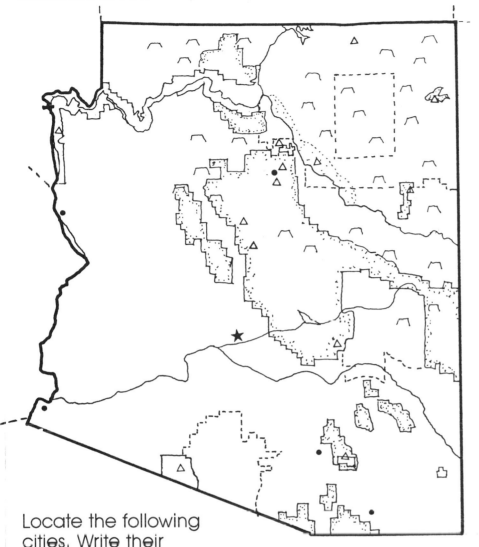

Legend:
- ★ State capital
- • City
- △ Points of Interest
- Plateaus
- National Forest
- National Park
- Indian Reservations

Write the names of the states, river and country that border Arizona in their correct locations on the map.

Color the Grand Canyon grey.

Words:
saguaro   canyon   desert
cactus   reservation

Locate the following cities. Write their numbers below next to their dots on the map.

1. Tucson   2. Phoenix   3. Flagstaff   4. Yuma   5. Tombstone   6. Lake Havasu City

Label the rivers, lakes and National Forests appropriately on the map. Mark an **X** on the Navajo Indian Reservation, a **Y** on the Papago Indian Reservation and a **Z** on the Fort Apache and San Carlos Indian Reservations. Circle the Hopi Indian Reservation.

Points of Interest: Locate the following places to see. Write their letters below next to the symbols that represent them.

A. Canyon de Chelly National Monument
B. Painted Desert
C. Petrified Forest National Park
D. Montezuma Castle National Monument
E. Tonto National Monument
F. Organ Pipe Cactus National Monument
G. Tuzigoot National Monument
H. Hoover Dam
I. Navajo National Monument
J. Saguaro National Monument
K. Walnut Canyon
L. Sunset Crater
M. Wupatki

Arkansas

Statehood: June 15, 1836 – 25th

Area: 53,104 square miles

Postal Abbreviation: AR

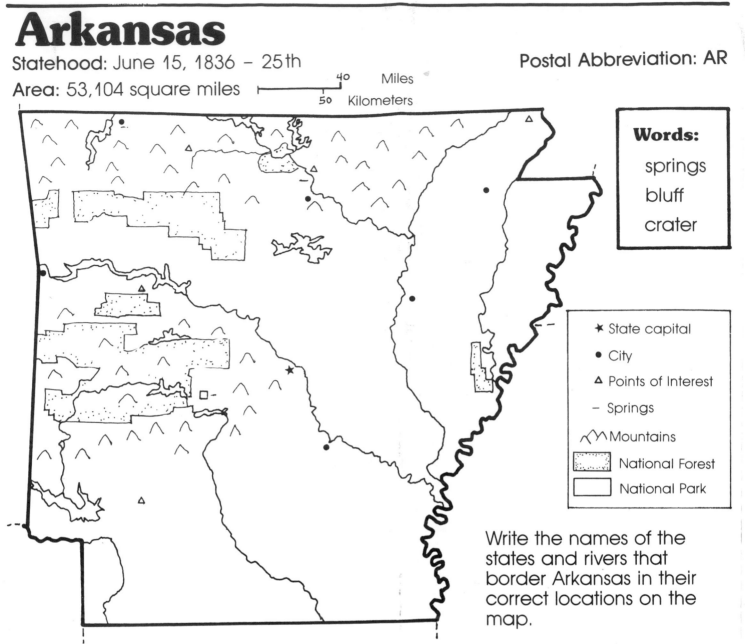

Words:

springs

bluff

crater

★ State capital
• City
△ Points of Interest
– Springs
⋀⋀ Mountains
National Forest
National Park

Write the names of the states and rivers that border Arkansas in their correct locations on the map.

Locate the following cities. Write their numbers below next to their dots on the map.

1. Little Rock **3.** Fort Smith **5.** Batesville **7.** Eureka Springs

2. Pine Bluff **4.** Newport **6.** Jonesboro

The capital is _____.

Label the rivers, lakes, mountain ranges and National Forests appropriately on the map.

Circle Hot Springs National Park, mark a line through Eureka Springs and mark an **X** on Blanchard Springs Caverns.

Points of Interest: Locate the following places to see. Write their letters below next to the symbols that represent them.

A. Magazine Mountain **C.** Crater of Diamonds **E.** Calico Rock

B. Dog Patch U.S.A. **D.** Chalk Bluff

California

Statehood: September 9, 1850 – 31st

Postal Abbreviation: CA

Area: 158,693 square miles

Miles

Kilometers

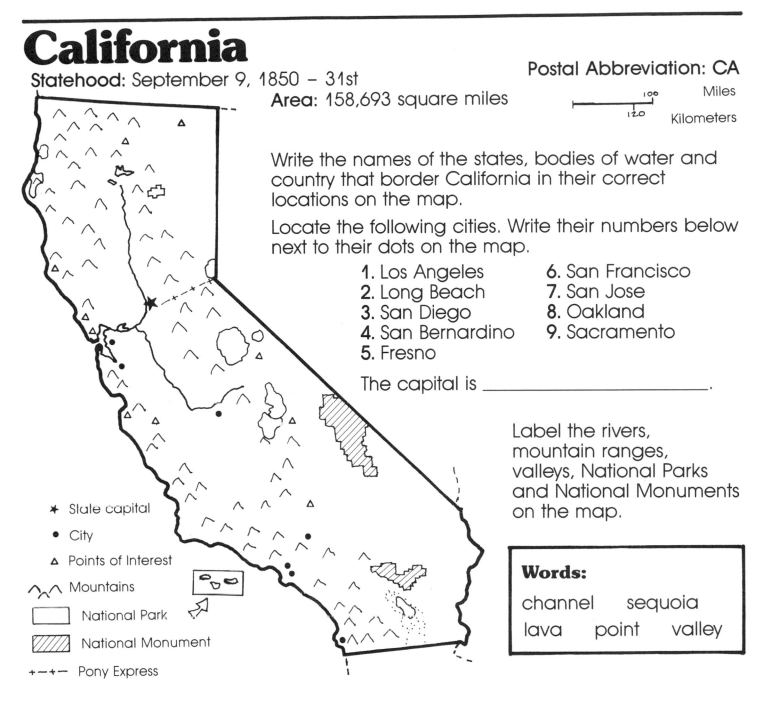

Write the names of the states, bodies of water and country that border California in their correct locations on the map.

Locate the following cities. Write their numbers below next to their dots on the map.

1. Los Angeles
2. Long Beach
3. San Diego
4. San Bernardino
5. Fresno
6. San Francisco
7. San Jose
8. Oakland
9. Sacramento

The capital is _____.

Label the rivers, mountain ranges, valleys, National Parks and National Monuments on the map.

Words:

channel   sequoia

lava   point   valley

Legend:
★ State capital
● City
△ Points of Interest
⌃⌃⌃ Mountains
▭ National Park
▨ National Monument
+—+— Pony Express

Trace over the Pony Express with orange. Write a **T** on Lake Tahoe, an **M** on Mono Lake and an **S** on Shasta Lake. Circle the Salton Sea. Mark an **X** on the Mohave Desert. Color the valleys green.

Points of Interest: Locate the following places to see. Write their letters below next to the symbols that represent them.

A. Golden Gate National Recreation Area
B. Pinnacles National Monument
C. Mount Shasta
D. Mount Whitney
E. Muir Woods National Monument

F. Devil's Post Pile National Monument
G. Monterey Peninsula
H. Edwards Air Force Base
I. Point Arena
J. Lava Beds National Monument

Colorado

Statehood: August 1, 1876 – 38th
Area: 104,247 square miles

Postal Abbreviation: CO

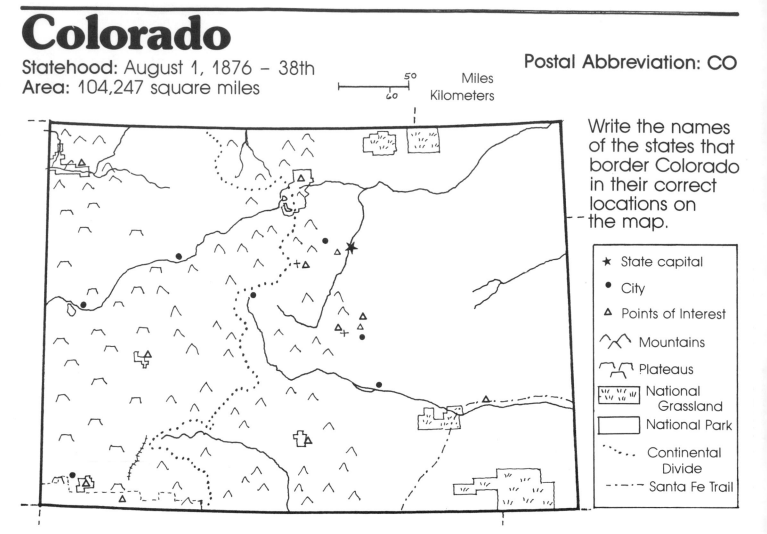

50 Miles
60 Kilometers

Write the names of the states that border Colorado in their correct locations on the map.

★ State capital
• City
△ Points of Interest
⌃⌃ Mountains
⌐⌐ Plateaus
National Grassland
National Park
⋯⋯ Continental Divide
-·-·- Santa Fe Trail

Locate the following cities. Write their numbers below next to their dots on the map.

1. Grand Junction   3. Cortez   5. Colorado Springs   7. Glenwood Springs
2. Denver   4. Pueblo   6. Boulder   8. Leadville

Label the mountain range, grasslands, rivers, creeks, reservoir, and lakes on the map.

Trace the Santa Fe Trail with red, the Continental Divide with green, the Royal Gorge with brown and the Narrow Guage Railroad with blue. Make an **X** to locate Durango and a **Y** for Silverton.

Points of Interest: Locate the following places. Write their letters below next to the symbols that represent them.

A. Mesa Verde National Park
B. Great Sand Dunes National Monument
C. Black Canyon of the Gunnison National Monument
D. Dinosaur National Monument
E. Rocky Mountain National Park
F. Ute Indian Reservation

G. U.S. Air Force Academy
H. Pike's Peak
I. Garden of the Gods
J. Bent's Fort
K. Central City
L. Mt. Evans

Words: peak   canyon   fork   mesa   pass

Connecticut

Statehood: January 9, 1788 – 5th

Area: 5009 square miles

Postal Abbreviation: CT

10 Miles
12 Kilometers

★ State capital   △ Points of Interest

● City

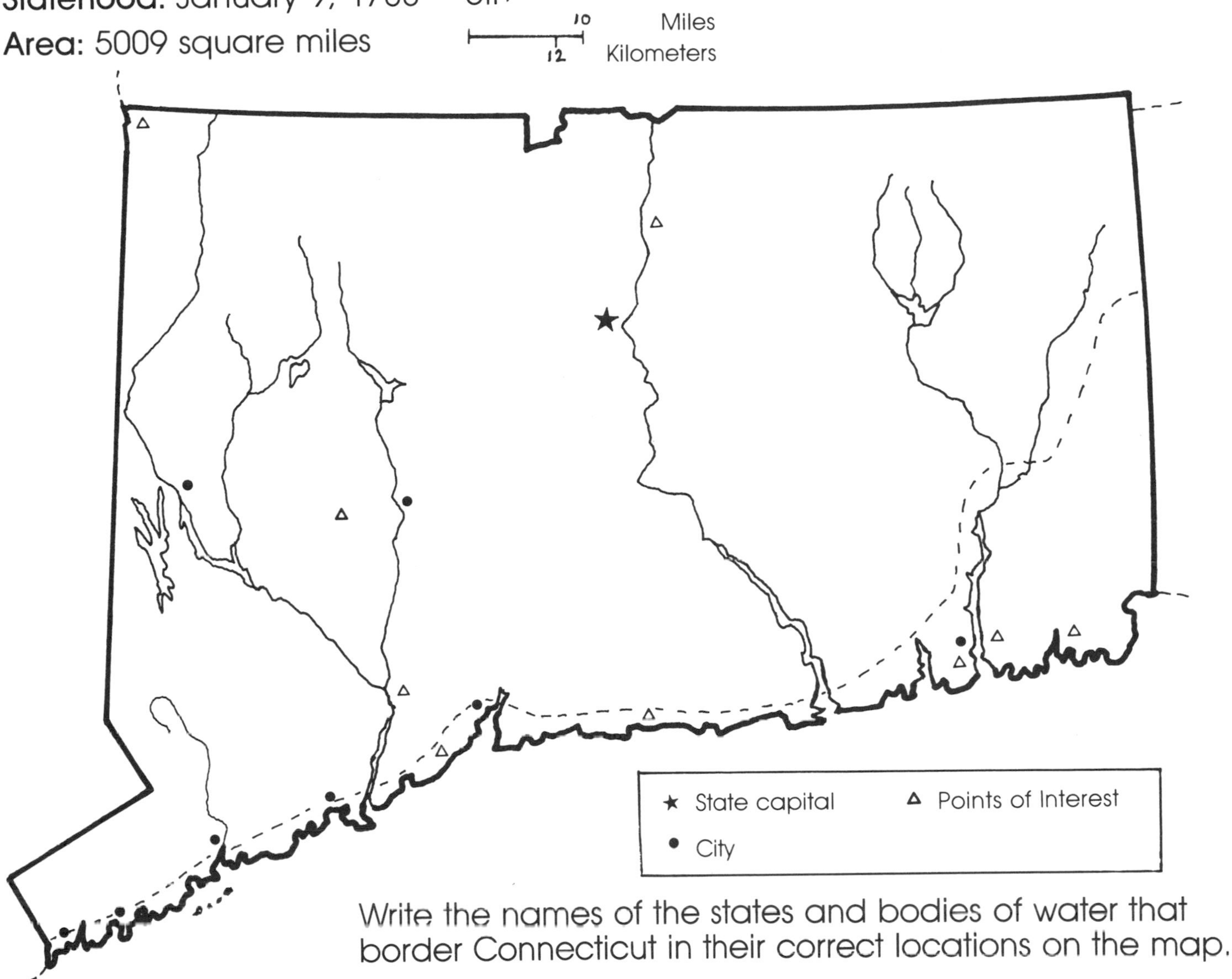

Write the names of the states and bodies of water that border Connecticut in their correct locations on the map.

Locate the following cities. Write their numbers below next to their dots on the map.

1. Stamford
2. Bridgeport
3. Hartford
4. New Haven
5. Waterbury
6. Greenwich
7. New London
8. New Milford
9. Norwalk

The capital is _____.

Label the rivers and lakes on the map. Trace over the Connecticut Turnpike with blue. Circle New Haven Harbor. Mark an **X** on the Norwalk Islands.

Points of Interest: Locate the following places. Write their letters below next to the symbols that represent them.

A. Old Town Mill
B. Fort Griswold and Groton Monument
C. Mystic Seaport
D. Mount Frissell
E. Whitfield House
F. Trolley Museums
G. Glebe House
H. Mansfield House

Words: hollow   harbor   sound   knoll

Delaware

Statehood: December 7, 1787 – 1st

Area: 2057 square miles

Postal Abbreviation: DE

⊢————————┤	10	Miles
	14	Kilometers

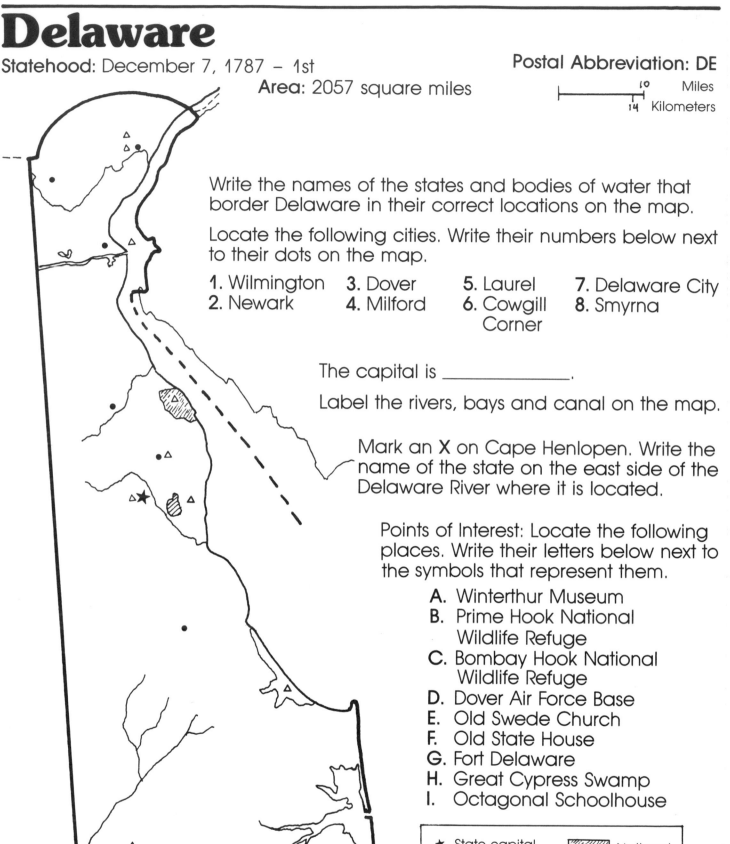

Write the names of the states and bodies of water that border Delaware in their correct locations on the map.

Locate the following cities. Write their numbers below next to their dots on the map.

1. Wilmington
2. Newark
3. Dover
4. Milford
5. Laurel
6. Cowgill Corner
7. Delaware City
8. Smyrna

The capital is _____.

Label the rivers, bays and canal on the map.

Mark an **X** on Cape Henlopen. Write the name of the state on the east side of the Delaware River where it is located.

Points of Interest: Locate the following places. Write their letters below next to the symbols that represent them.

A. Winterthur Museum
B. Prime Hook National Wildlife Refuge
C. Bombay Hook National Wildlife Refuge
D. Dover Air Force Base
E. Old Swede Church
F. Old State House
G. Fort Delaware
H. Great Cypress Swamp
I. Octagonal Schoolhouse

★ State capital
• City
△ Points of Interest
▨ National Wildlife Refuge

Words: bay   cape   swamp   canal   cypress   hook

Florida

Statehood: March 3, 1845 – 27th

Area: 58,560 square miles

Postal Abbreviation: FL

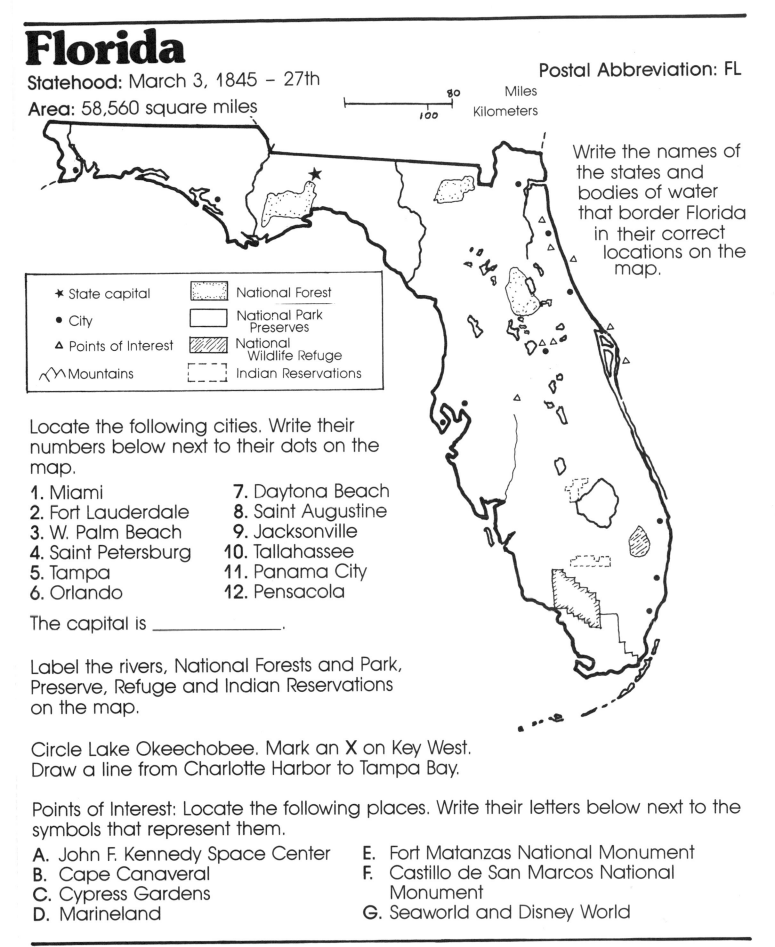

Write the names of the states and bodies of water that border Florida in their correct locations on the map.

Legend:
- ★ State capital
- • City
- △ Points of Interest
- ⋀⋀ Mountains
- National Forest
- National Park Preserves
- National Wildlife Refuge
- Indian Reservations

Locate the following cities. Write their numbers below next to their dots on the map.

1. Miami
2. Fort Lauderdale
3. W. Palm Beach
4. Saint Petersburg
5. Tampa
6. Orlando
7. Daytona Beach
8. Saint Augustine
9. Jacksonville
10. Tallahassee
11. Panama City
12. Pensacola

The capital is _____.

Label the rivers, National Forests and Park, Preserve, Refuge and Indian Reservations on the map.

Circle Lake Okeechobee. Mark an **X** on Key West.
Draw a line from Charlotte Harbor to Tampa Bay.

Points of Interest: Locate the following places. Write their letters below next to the symbols that represent them.

A. John F. Kennedy Space Center
B. Cape Canaveral
C. Cypress Gardens
D. Marineland
E. Fort Matanzas National Monument
F. Castillo de San Marcos National Monument
G. Seaworld and Disney World

Words: key   strait   gulf   harbor

Georgia

Statehood: January 2, 1788 – 4th
Area: 58,876 square miles

Postal Abbreviation: GA

50 Miles
70 Kilometers

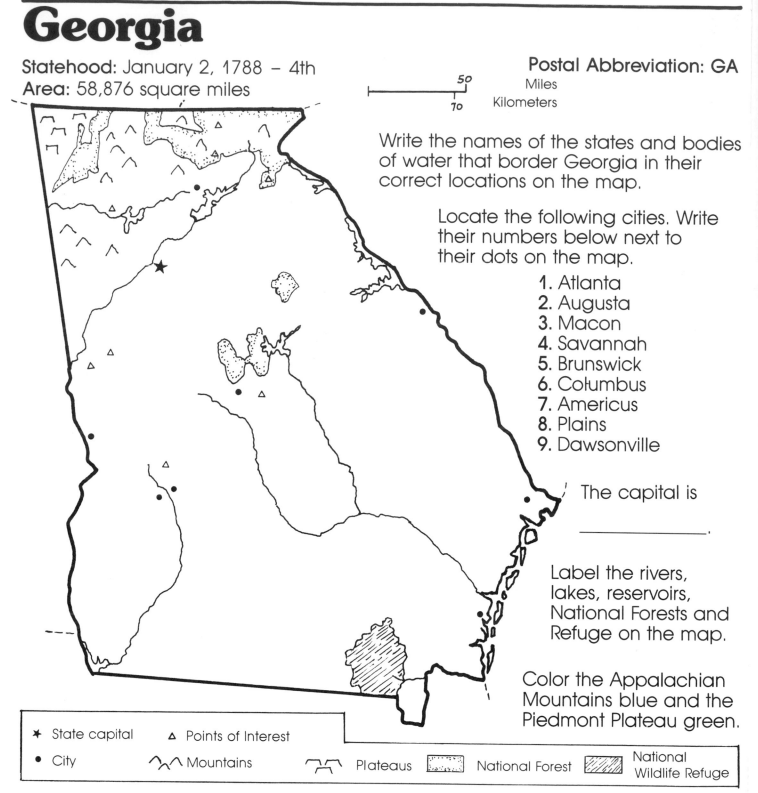

Write the names of the states and bodies of water that border Georgia in their correct locations on the map.

Locate the following cities. Write their numbers below next to their dots on the map.

1. Atlanta
2. Augusta
3. Macon
4. Savannah
5. Brunswick
6. Columbus
7. Americus
8. Plains
9. Dawsonville

The capital is

_____.

Label the rivers, lakes, reservoirs, National Forests and Refuge on the map.

Color the Appalachian Mountains blue and the Piedmont Plateau green.

★ State capital   △ Points of Interest

● City   ⌃⌃⌃ Mountains   ⊓⊔ Plateaus   National Forest   National Wildlife Refuge

Points of Interest: Locate the following places. Write their letters below next to the symbols that represent them.

A. Andersonville National Historic Site
B. Callaway Gardens
C. Little White House
D. Etowah Mounds

E. Dahlonega Gold Museum
F. Toccoa Falls
G. Brasstown Bald Mountain
H. Ocmulgee National Monument

Words: falls   mound

Hawaii

Statehood: August 21, 1959 – 50th

Area: 6450 square miles

Postal Abbreviation: HI

40 Miles
50 Kilometers

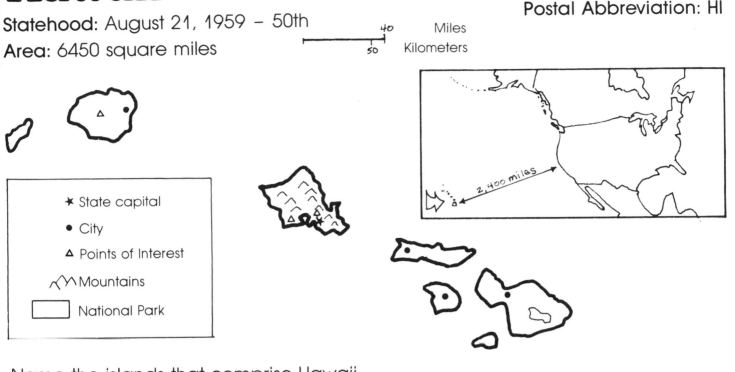

* ★ State capital
* ● City
* △ Points of Interest
* ᐱᐱ Mountains
* ▭ National Park

Name the islands that comprise Hawaii and the body of water that surrounds them.

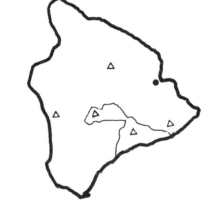

Locate the following cities. Write their numbers below next to their dots on the map.

1. Hilo   3. Koele   5. Honolulu
2. Wailuku 4. Maunaloa 6. Wailua

The capital is _____.

Label the mountain ranges and channels on the map.

Color Hawaii Volcanoes National Park green and Haleakala National Park orange.

Points of Interest: Locate the following places. Write their letters below next to the symbols that represent them.

A. Kalapana Black Sand Beach   E. Royal Mausoleum
B. Kealakekua Bay   F. Mauna Loa Volcano
C. Pearl Harbor   G. Kilauea Crater
D. Waimea Canyon   H. Mauna Kea

Words: crater   island   volcano   beach   atoll

Idaho

Statehood: July 3, 1890 – 43rd

Area: 83,557 square miles

Postal Abbreviation: ID

50 Miles
60 Kilometers

Legend:
- ★ State capital
- ● City
- △ Points of Interest
- ∧∧ Mountains
- Plateaus
- Indian Reservations
- Continental Divide
- Oregon Trail
- Lewis and Clark Expedition

Write the names of the states, country, mountain range and body of water that border Idaho in their correct locations on the map.

Locate the following cities. Write their numbers below next to their dots on the map.

1. Boise   3. Ketchum   5. Twin Falls
2. Idaho Falls 4. Pocatello   6. Lewiston

The capital is _____.

Label the lakes, rivers, mountain range, plateau and Indian Reservations on the map.

Trace over the Continental Divide with blue, Lewis and Clark Expedition with orange, and the Oregon trail with brown.

Points of Interest: Locate the following places. Write their letters below next to the symbols that represent them.

A. Cataldo Mission
B. Hells Canyon
C. Fort Boise
D. National Reactor Testing Station
E. Craters of the Moon National Monument
F. Sun Valley
G. Cities of Rock (2)
H. Pilot Knob
I. Shoshone Falls
J. Balanced Rock
K. Old Fort Hall

Words: salmon   sawtooth   knob

12

Illinois

Statehood: December 3, 1818 – 21st
Area: 56,400 square miles

Postal Abbreviation: IL

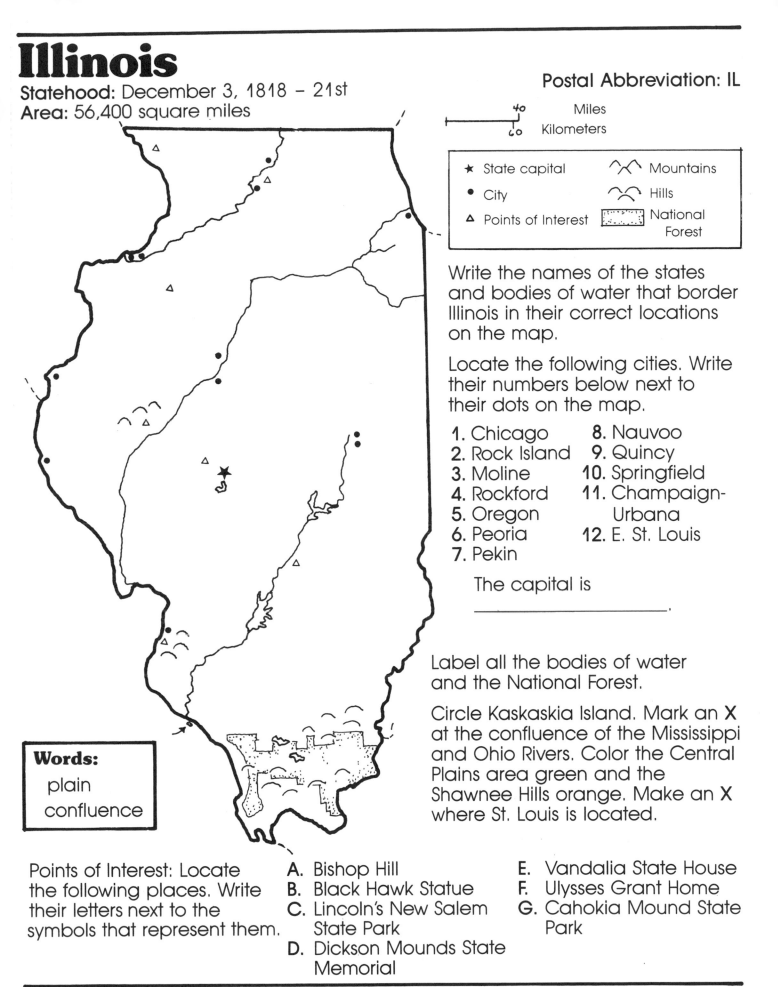

Miles 40
Kilometers 60

★ State capital   ⌃⌃⌃ Mountains
● City   ⌃⌃ Hills
△ Points of Interest   ▭ National Forest

Write the names of the states and bodies of water that border Illinois in their correct locations on the map.

Locate the following cities. Write their numbers below next to their dots on the map.

1. Chicago   8. Nauvoo
2. Rock Island 9. Quincy
3. Moline   10. Springfield
4. Rockford   11. Champaign-
5. Oregon   Urbana
6. Peoria   12. E. St. Louis
7. Pekin

The capital is

_____.

Label all the bodies of water and the National Forest.

Circle Kaskaskia Island. Mark an **X** at the confluence of the Mississippi and Ohio Rivers. Color the Central Plains area green and the Shawnee Hills orange. Make an **X** where St. Louis is located.

Words:
plain
confluence

Points of Interest: Locate the following places. Write their letters next to the symbols that represent them.

A. Bishop Hill
B. Black Hawk Statue
C. Lincoln's New Salem State Park
D. Dickson Mounds State Memorial

E. Vandalia State House
F. Ulysses Grant Home
G. Cahokia Mound State Park

Indiana

Statehood: December 11, 1816 – 19th

Postal Abbreviation: IN

Area: 36,291 square miles

30 Miles
40 Kilometers

Words:
Hoosier
creek

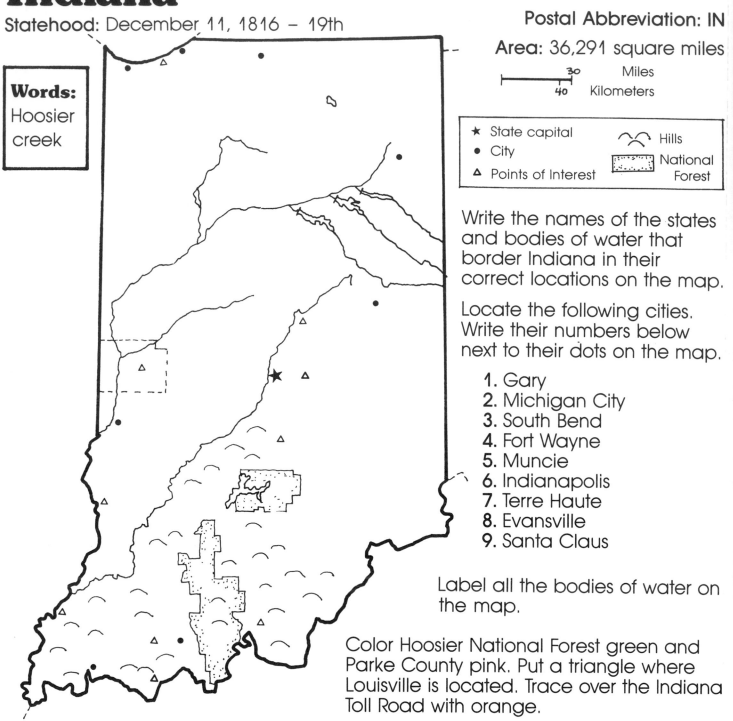

★ State capital
• City
△ Points of Interest

∩∩ Hills
National Forest

Write the names of the states and bodies of water that border Indiana in their correct locations on the map.

Locate the following cities. Write their numbers below next to their dots on the map.

1. Gary
2. Michigan City
3. South Bend
4. Fort Wayne
5. Muncie
6. Indianapolis
7. Terre Haute
8. Evansville
9. Santa Claus

Label all the bodies of water on the map.

Color Hoosier National Forest green and Parke County pink. Put a triangle where Louisville is located. Trace over the Indiana Toll Road with orange.

Points of Interest: Locate the following places. Write their letters below next to the symbols that represent them.

A. Lincoln Boyhood National Memorial
B. Wyandotte Cave
C. William Henry Harrison Home
D. One of thirty covered bridges in country
E. Indiana Dunes National Lakeshore

F. Brown County Art Galleries
G. Conner Prairie Pioneer Settlement
H. James Whitcomb Riley Home
I. Lincoln Pioneer Village
J. New Harmony Historic District

Iowa

Statehood: December 28, 1846 – 29th

Area: 56,290 square miles

Postal Abbreviation: IA

Miles

Kilometers

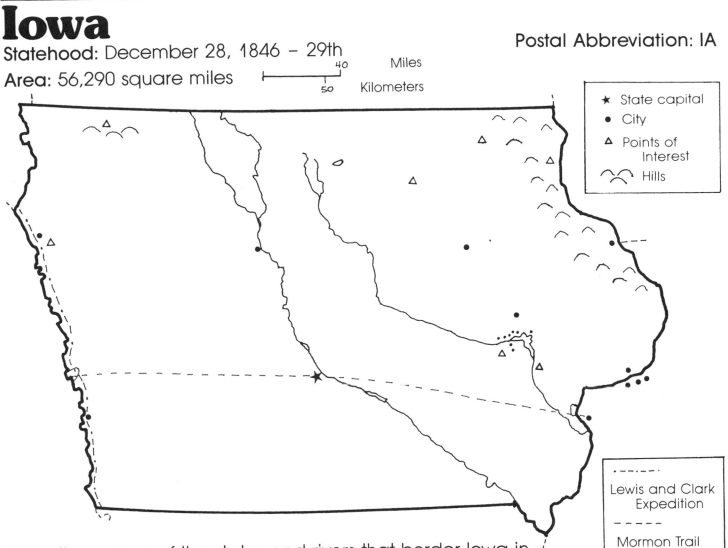

★ State capital
● City
△ Points of Interest
⌒⌒ Hills

Lewis and Clark Expedition

Mormon Trail

Write the names of the states and rivers that border Iowa in their correct locations on the map.

Locate the following cities. Write their numbers below next to their dots on the map.

1. Des Moines
2. Davenport
3. Nauvoo (IL)
4. Dubuque
5. Fort Dodge
6. Sioux City
7. Council Bluffs
8. Cedar Rapids
9. Waterloo

Label the rivers lake, and the three cities across the river from Davenport.

Mark an **X** at the confluence of the Big Sioux and the Missouri Rivers, and a **Y** at the confluence of the Mississippi and Des Moines Rivers. Trace over the Lewis and Clark Expedition with orange and the Mormon Trail with black.

Points of Interest: Locate the following places. Write their letters below next to the symbols that represent them.

A. Effigy Mounds National Monument
B. Ocheyedan Mound
C. Amana Colonies
D. Herbert Hoover National Historic Site
E. Little Brown Church
F. Dvorak Memorial
G. Floyd Monument

Words: effigy expedition

Kansas

Statehood: January 29, 1861 – 34th

Area: 82,264 square miles

Postal Abbreviation: KS

40 Miles
50 Kilometers

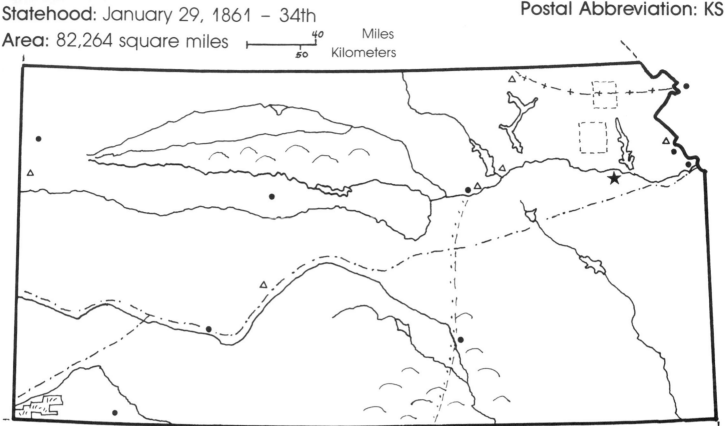

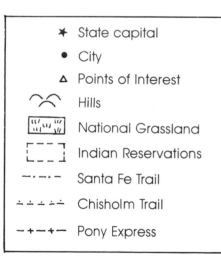

★ State capital
● City
△ Points of Interest
⌒⌒ Hills
National Grassland
Indian Reservations
–·–·– Santa Fe Trail
–·–·– Chisholm Trail
–+–+– Pony Express

Write the names of the states and body of water that border Kansas in their correct location on the map.

Locate the following cities. Write their numbers below next to their dots on the map.

1. Dodge City   4. Leavenworth   7. Goodland
2. Wichita   5. Abilene   8. Liberal
3. Topeka   6. Hays   9. Kansas City, KS

The capital is _____.

Label the bodies of water, Smoky Hills, Flint Hills and grassland area on the map.

Mark an **X** on St. Joseph, Missouri. Color the Indian Reservations green. Trace the Santa Fe Trail red, the Pony Express brown and the Chisholm Trail grey.

Points of Interest: Locate the following places. Write their letters below next to the symbols that represent them.

A. Mount Sunflower
B. Fort Leavenworth
C. Fort Larned National Historic Site

D. Eisenhower Library and Museum
E. Fort Riley
F. Hollenberg Station

Words: flint   hill

Kentucky

Statehood: June 1, 1792 – 15th

Area: 40,395 square miles

Postal Abbreviation: KY

40 Miles
60 Kilometers

Words:
dam
hollow
gap

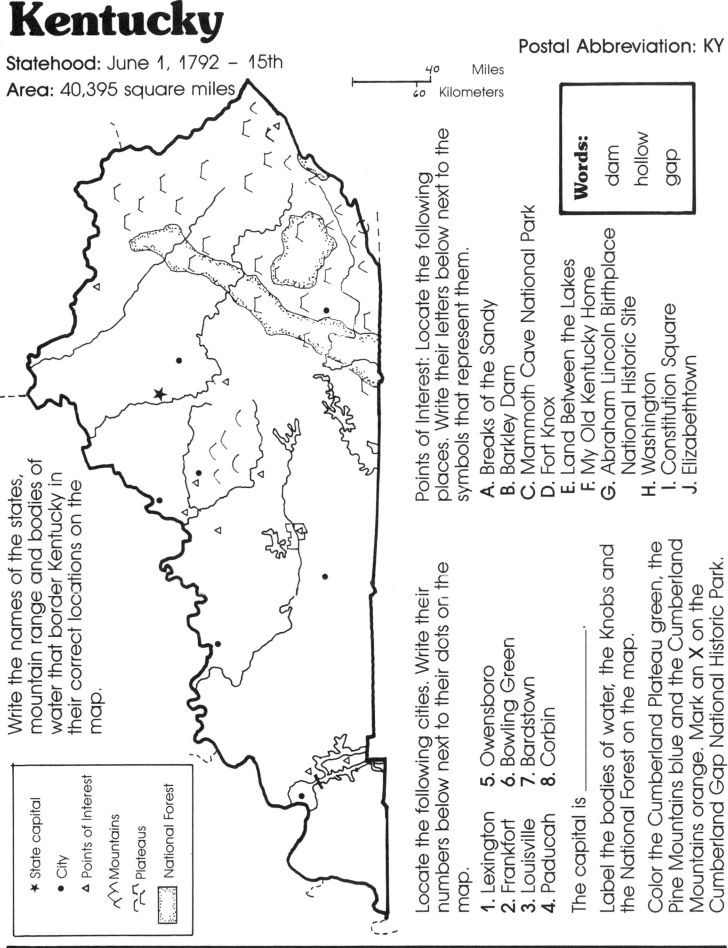

Write the names of the states, mountain range and bodies of water that border Kentucky in their correct locations on the map.

★ State capital
● City
▲ Points of Interest
ᴧᴧᴧ Mountains
ᴦᴖᴦ Plateaus
▭ National Forest

Points of Interest: Locate the following places. Write their letters below next to the symbols that represent them.

A. Breaks of the Sandy
B. Barkley Dam
C. Mammoth Cave National Park
D. Fort Knox
E. Land Between the Lakes
F. My Old Kentucky Home
G. Abraham Lincoln Birthplace National Historic Site
H. Washington
I. Constitution Square
J. Elizabethtown

Locate the following cities. Write their numbers below next to their dots on the map.

1. Lexington
2. Frankfort
3. Louisville
4. Paducah
5. Owensboro
6. Bowling Green
7. Bardstown
8. Corbin

The capital is _____

Label the bodies of water, the Knobs and the National Forest on the map.

Color the Cumberland Plateau green, the Pine Mountains blue and the Cumberland Mountains orange. Mark an X on the Cumberland Gap National Historic Park.

Louisiana

Statehood: April 30, 1812 – 18th
Area: 48,523 square miles

Postal Abbreviation: LA

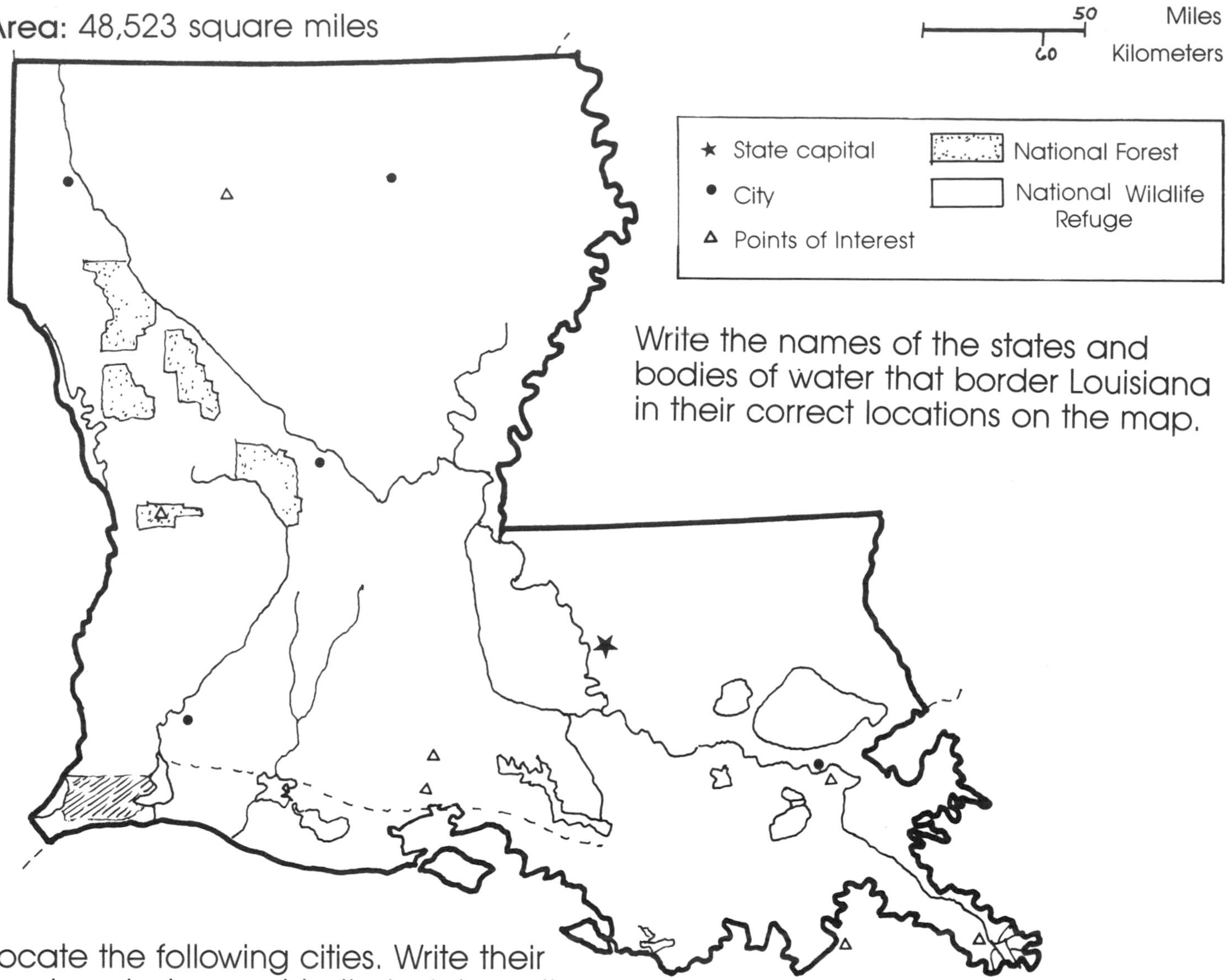

50 Miles
60 Kilometers

★ State capital   [⋯] National Forest
● City   [ ] National Wildlife Refuge
△ Points of Interest

Write the names of the states and bodies of water that border Louisiana in their correct locations on the map.

Locate the following cities. Write their numbers below next to their dots on the map.

1. New Orleans   4. Monroe
2. Baton Rouge   5. Shreveport
3. Lake Charles   6. Alexandria

Label the lakes, reservoir, National Forest and rivers on the map.

Trace over the Intercoastal Waterway with red. Color the Sabine National Wildlife Refuge green. Draw a line from Lake Borgne to Barataria Bay to Vermillion Bay.

Points of Interest: Locate the following places. Write their letters below next to the symbols that represent them.

A. Evangeline Oak
B. Avery Island
C. Driskill Mountain
D. Mississippi Delta
E. Jean Lafitte National Historic Park and Reserve
F. Grand Isle
G. Fort Polk Military Reservation

Words: bayou   delta

Maine

Statehood: March 15, 1820 – 23rd
Area: 33,215 square miles

Postal Abbreviation: ME

30 Miles
40 Kilometers

Label the National Forest, bodies of water and main mountain range on the map.

Write the names of the state, bodies of water and provinces of Canada that border Maine in their correct locations on the map.

Locate the following cities. Write their numbers below next to their dots on the map.

1. Bar Harbor
2. Lewiston
3. Portland
4. Augusta
5. Bangor
6. Waterville

The capital is

_____

★ State capital
● City
△ Points of Interest
ⵣⵣ Mountains
National Forest

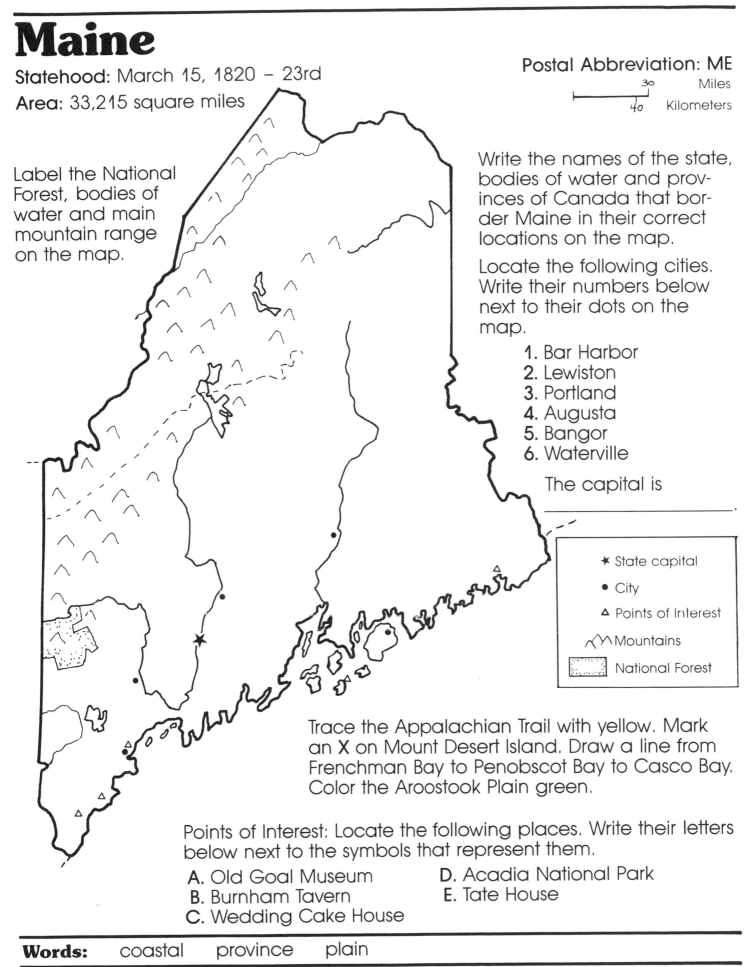

Trace the Appalachian Trail with yellow. Mark an **X** on Mount Desert Island. Draw a line from Frenchman Bay to Penobscot Bay to Casco Bay. Color the Aroostook Plain green.

Points of Interest: Locate the following places. Write their letters below next to the symbols that represent them.

A. Old Goal Museum
B. Burnham Tavern
C. Wedding Cake House
D. Acadia National Park
E. Tate House

Words: coastal   province   plain

Maryland

Statehood: April 28, 1788 – 7th

Area: 10,577 square miles

Postal Abbreviation: MD

25 Miles
30 Kilometers

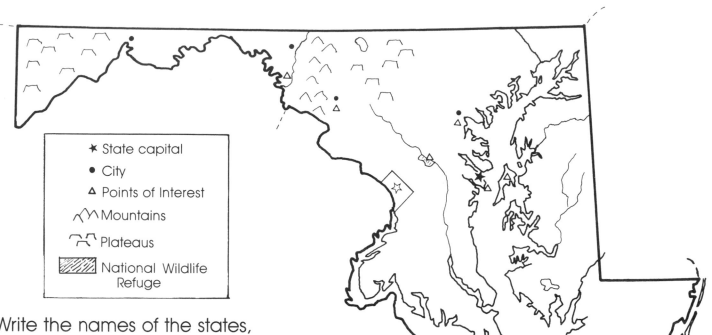

Legend:
- ★ State capital
- • City
- △ Points of Interest
- ⋀⋀ Mountains
- ⌐⌐ Plateaus
- ▨ National Wildlife Refuge

Write the names of the states, bodies of water and a District that border Maryland in their correct locations on the map.

Locate the following cities. Write their numbers below next to their dots on the map.

1. Baltimore
2. Washington, D.C.
3. Annapolis
4. Cumberland
5. Hagerstown
6. Frederick

The capital is _____.

Label the two mountain ranges, two plateaus and the rivers on the map.

Color all of Chesapeake Bay blue. Color the District of Columbia red. Mark an **X** on the nation's capital.

Points of Interest: Locate the following places. Write their letters below next to the symbols that represent them.

A. Kent Island
B. Assateague Island National Sea Shore
C. Antietam National Battlefield Site
D. Barbara Fritchie House
E. U.S. Naval Academy
F. Fort McHenry
G. Patuxent Wildlife Refuge

Words: branch district

Massachusetts

Statehood: February 6, 1788 – 6th

Area: 8,257 square miles

Postal Abbreviation: MA

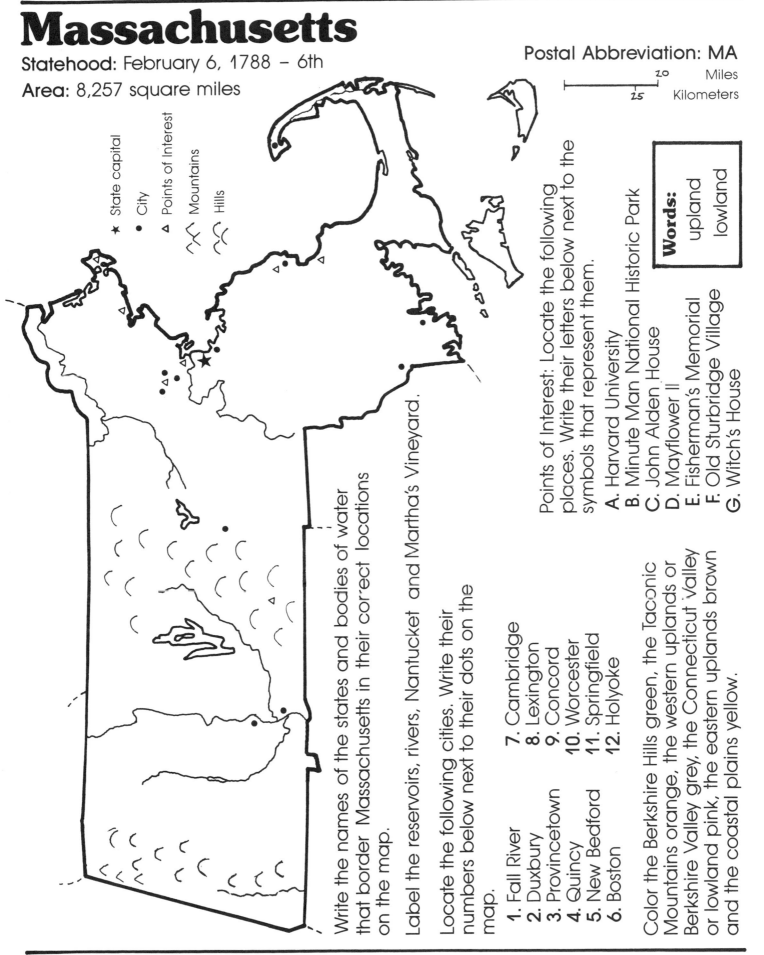

State capital
City
Points of Interest
Mountains
Hills

Words: upland lowland

Points of Interest: Locate the following places. Write their letters below next to the symbols that represent them.

A. Harvard University
B. Minute Man National Historic Park
C. John Alden House
D. Mayflower II
E. Fisherman's Memorial
F. Old Sturbridge Village
G. Witch's House

Write the names of the states and bodies of water that border Massachusetts in their correct locations on the map.

Label the reservoirs, rivers, Nantucket and Martha's Vineyard.

Locate the following cities. Write their numbers below next to their dots on the map.

1. Fall River
2. Duxbury
3. Provincetown
4. Quincy
5. New Bedford
6. Boston
7. Cambridge
8. Lexington
9. Concord
10. Worcester
11. Springfield
12. Holyoke

Color the Berkshire Hills green, the Taconic Mountains orange, the western uplands or Berkshire Valley grey, the Connecticut Valley or lowland pink, the eastern uplands brown and the coastal plains yellow.

Michigan

Statehood: January 26, 1837 – 26th

Postal Abbreviation: MI

Area: 58,216 square miles

60 Miles

80 Kilometers

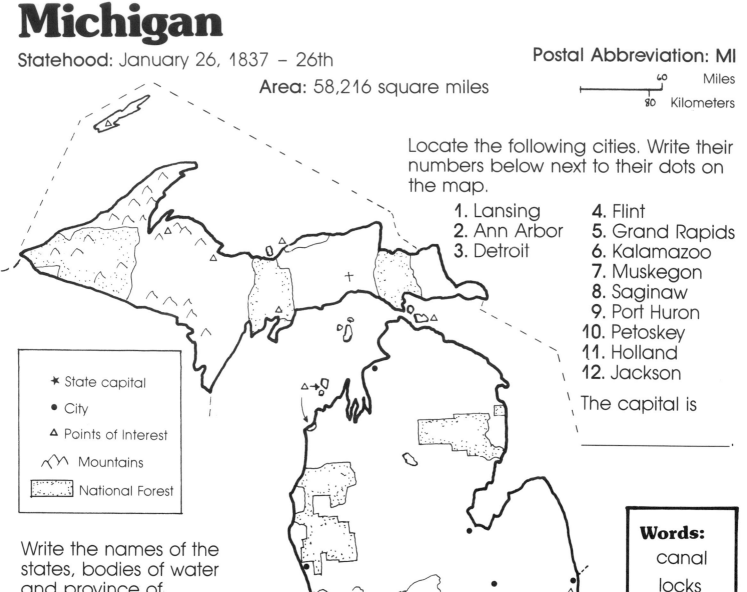

Locate the following cities. Write their numbers below next to their dots on the map.

1. Lansing
2. Ann Arbor
3. Detroit
4. Flint
5. Grand Rapids
6. Kalamazoo
7. Muskegon
8. Saginaw
9. Port Huron
10. Petoskey
11. Holland
12. Jackson

The capital is

_____

Legend:
- ★ State capital
- ● City
- △ Points of Interest
- ⋀⋁ Mountains
- National Forest

Words:
canal
locks

Write the names of the states, bodies of water and province of Canada that border Michigan in their correct locations on the map.

Label the National Forests, bodies of water and mountain ranges.

Color the upper peninsula orange and the lower peninsula red. Circle Mackinac Island. Mark an **X** on Beaver Island. Draw a line through the Soo Canal and Locks.

Points of Interest: Locate the following places. Write their letters below next to the symbols that represent them.

A. Big Spring
B. Fort Michilimackinac
C. Greenfield Village
D. Isle Royale National Park
E. Sleeping Bear Dunes National Lakeshore
F. U.S. Ski Hall of Fame
G. Pictured Rocks National Lakeshore
H. L'Anse Indian Reservation

Minnesota

Statehood: May 11, 1858 – 32nd

Postal Abbreviation: MN

Area: 84,068 square miles

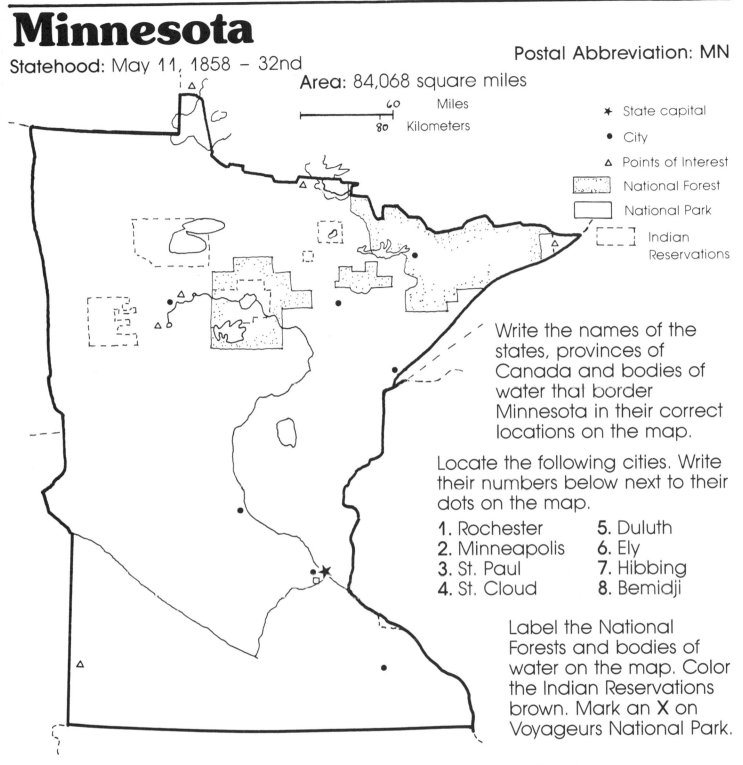

Miles 60
Kilometers 80

* State capital
• City
△ Points of Interest
National Forest
National Park
Indian Reservations

Write the names of the states, provinces of Canada and bodies of water that border Minnesota in their correct locations on the map.

Locate the following cities. Write their numbers below next to their dots on the map.

1. Rochester   5. Duluth
2. Minneapolis   6. Ely
3. St. Paul   7. Hibbing
4. St. Cloud   8. Bemidji

Label the National Forests and bodies of water on the map. Color the Indian Reservations brown. Mark an **X** on Voyageurs National Park.

Points of Interest: Locate the following places. Write their letters below next to the symbols that represent them.

A. The source of the Mississippi River
B. Pipestone National Monument
C. Grand Portage National Monument
D. Paul Bunyan and Babe statues

E. Northernmost Point of U.S. other than Alaska
F. International Falls

Words: international   portage   source

Mississippi

Statehood: December 10, 1817 – 20th

Postal Abbreviation: MS

Area: 47,716 square miles

30 Miles
40 Kilometers

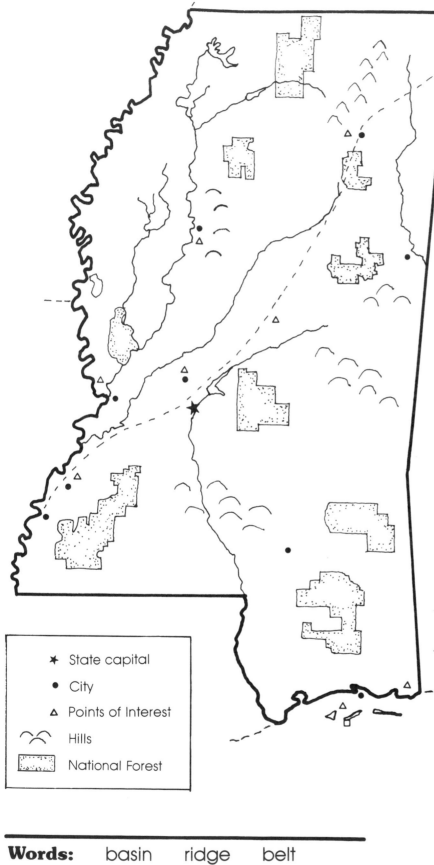

Write the names of the states and bodies of water that border Mississippi in their correct locations on the map.

Locate the following cities. Write their numbers below next to their dots on the map.

1. Natchez
2. Fayette
3. Jackson
4. Flora
5. Vicksburg
6. Greenwood
7. Tupelo
8. Columbus
9. Hattiesburg
10. Biloxi

The capital is _____.

Label the bodies of water and National Forests on the map.

Color the Pine Hill Region green, the Red Hill Region red, the Black Belt Region black, the Bluff Hill Region tan and the Pontoto Ridge orange. Trace the Nachez Trace Parkway with a pencil. Circle the Yazoo Basin.

Points of Interest: Locate the following places. Write their letters below next to the symbols that represent them.

A. Vicksburg National Military Park
B. Elvis Presley Birthplace
C. Petrified Forest
D. Choctaw Indian Reservation
E. Florewood River Plantation
F. Mount Locust
G. Ship Island
H. Old Spanish Fort

Legend:
★ State capital
● City
△ Points of Interest
⌒⌒ Hills
▨ National Forest

Words: basin   ridge   belt

Map Skills IF8751

24

© 1990 Instructional Fair, Inc.

Missouri

Statehood: August 10, 1821 – 24th

Area: 69,686 square miles

Postal Abbreviation: MO

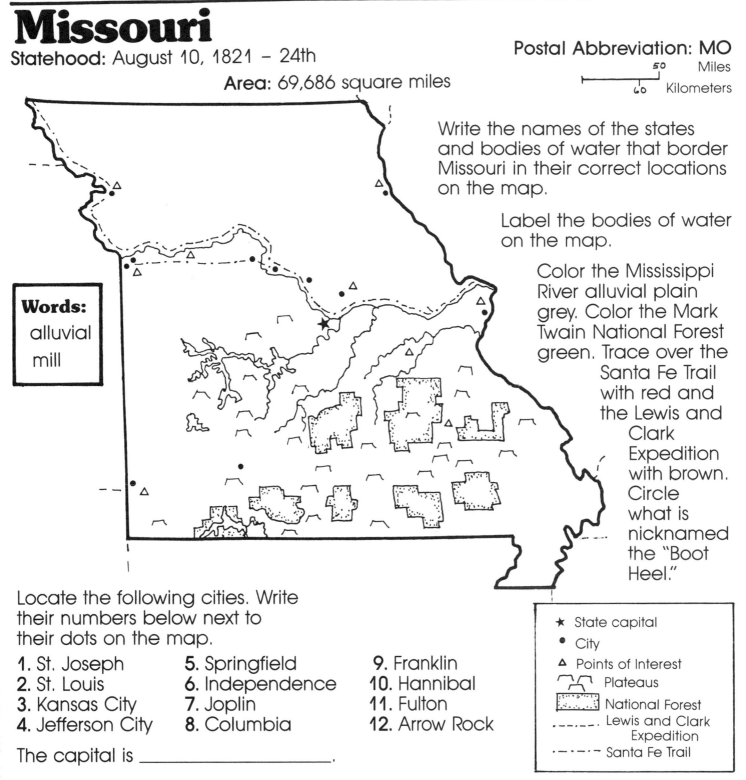

Write the names of the states and bodies of water that border Missouri in their correct locations on the map.

Label the bodies of water on the map.

Color the Mississippi River alluvial plain grey. Color the Mark Twain National Forest green. Trace over the Santa Fe Trail with red and the Lewis and Clark Expedition with brown. Circle what is nicknamed the "Boot Heel."

Words:
alluvial
mill

Legend:
★ State capital
• City
△ Points of Interest
⌒ Plateaus
▦ National Forest
·——— Lewis and Clark Expedition
·—·—· Santa Fe Trail

Locate the following cities. Write their numbers below next to their dots on the map.

1. St. Joseph
2. St. Louis
3. Kansas City
4. Jefferson City
5. Springfield
6. Independence
7. Joplin
8. Columbia
9. Franklin
10. Hannibal
11. Fulton
12. Arrow Rock

The capital is _____.

Points of Interest: Locate the following places. Write their letters below next to the symbols that represent them.

A. George Washington Carver National Monument
B. Winston Churchill Memorial and Library
C. Pony Express Stables
D. Mark Twain Home and Museum
E. Meramec Caverns
F. Jefferson National Expansion Memorial—The Gateway Arch
G. Anderson House
H. Truman Library
I. Elephant Rocks

Montana

Statehood: November 8, 1889 – 41st

Area: 147,138 square miles

Postal Abbreviation: MT

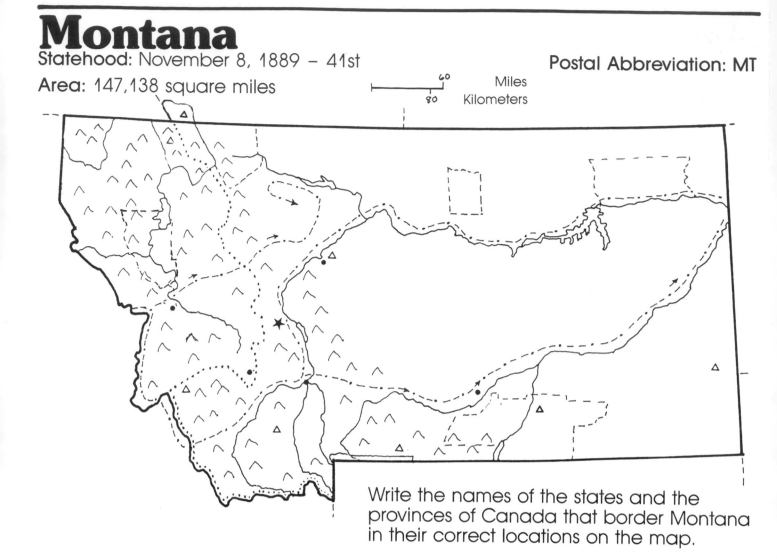

Write the names of the states and the provinces of Canada that border Montana in their correct locations on the map.

Locate the following cities. Write their numbers below next to their dots on the map.

1. Missoula
2. Helena
3. Great Falls
4. Butte
5. Three Forks
6. Billings

The capital is _____.

Points of Interest: Locate the following places. Write their letters below next to the symbols that represent them.

A. Virginia City
B. Giant Springs
C. Granite Peak
D. Big Hole Battlefield National Monument
E. Glacier National Park
F. Waterton Glacier International Peace Park
G. Custer Battlefield National Monument
H. Medicine Rocks

Legend:
- ✱ State capital
- ● City
- △ Points of Interest
- ⌃⌃ Mountains
- Indian Reservations
- Continental Divide
- Lewis and Clark Expedition

Label the bodies of water, mountain range and Indian Reservation on the map.

Trace over the Lewis and Clark Expedition with brown and the Continental Divide with blue.

Words: butte   granite

Nebraska

Statehood: March 1, 1867 – 37th

Area: 77,227 square miles

Postal Abbreviation: NE

Words:
agate
fossil

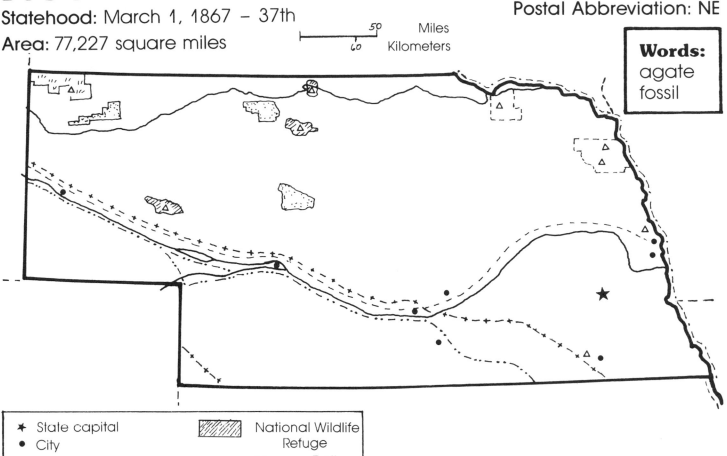

50 Miles

60 Kilometers

Legend:
- ✦ State capital
- ● City
- △ Points of Interest
- ▨ National Wildlife Refuge
- National Forest
- National Grassland
- Indian Reservations
- - - - - Mormon Trail
- -··-··- Oregon Trail
- -··-··- Lewis and Clark Expedition
- -+-+- Pony Express

Write the names of the states and the body of water that border Nebraska in their correct locations on the map.

Locate the following cities. Write their numbers below next to their dots on the map.

1. Scottsbluff
2. Hastings
3. Lincoln
4. Omaha
5. Bellevue

6. Kearney
7. Grand Island
8. North Platte
9. Beatrice

The capital is _____.

Label the bodies of water, National Forests and National Grasslands on the map.

Trace over the Oregon Trail with green, the Morman Trail with purple, the Pony Express with orange and the Lewis and Clark Expedition with brown.

Points of Interest: Locate the following places. Write their letters below next to the symbols that represent them.

A. Homestead National Monument of America
B. Omaha Indian Reservation
C. Winnebago Indian Reservation
D. Santee Indian Reservation
E. Toadstool Park
F. Valentine National Wildlife Refuge
G. Fort Niobrara National Wildlife Refuge
H. Crescent Lake National Wildlife Refuge
I. Boys Town

Nevada

Statehood: October 31, 1864 – 36th

Area: 110,540 square miles

Postal Abbreviation: NV

50 Miles

60 Kilometers

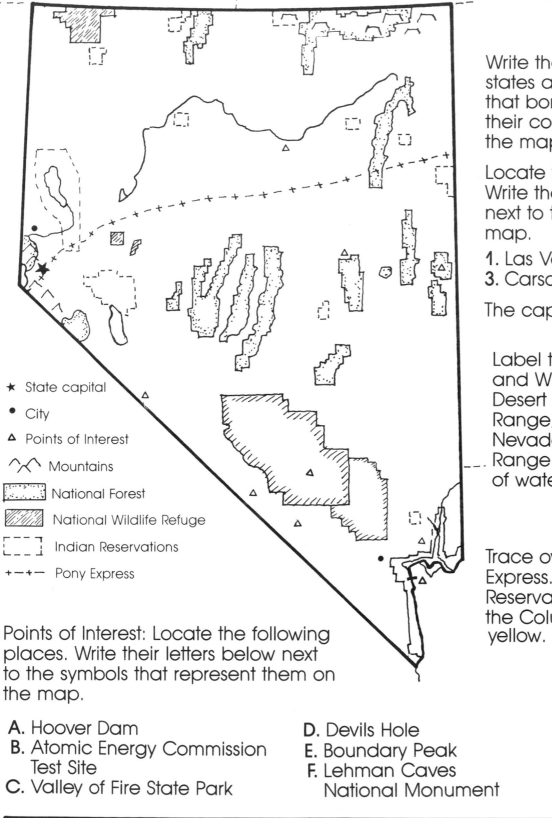

Write the names of the states and bodies of water that border Nevada in their correct locations on the map.

Locate the following cities. Write their numbers below next to their dots on the map.

1. Las Vegas   2. Reno
3. Carson City

The capital is _____

Label the National Forests and Wildlife Refuges, the Desert National Wildlife Range, the Sierra Nevada Mountain Range and the bodies of water on the map.

Trace over the Pony Express. Color the Indian Reservation brown. Color the Columbia Plateau yellow.

Legend:
- ★ State capital
- ● City
- △ Points of Interest
- ⌃⌃ Mountains
- National Forest
- National Wildlife Refuge
- Indian Reservations
- +—+— Pony Express

Points of Interest: Locate the following places. Write their letters below next to the symbols that represent them on the map.

A. Hoover Dam
B. Atomic Energy Commission Test Site
C. Valley of Fire State Park

D. Devils Hole
E. Boundary Peak
F. Lehman Caves National Monument

G. Ghost Towns: Rhyolite and Hamilton
H. Geyser Basin

Words: atomic   geyser   basin   range

New Hampshire

Statehood: June 21, 1788 – 9th
Area: 9,304 square miles

Postal Abbreviation: NH

20 Miles
24 Kilometers

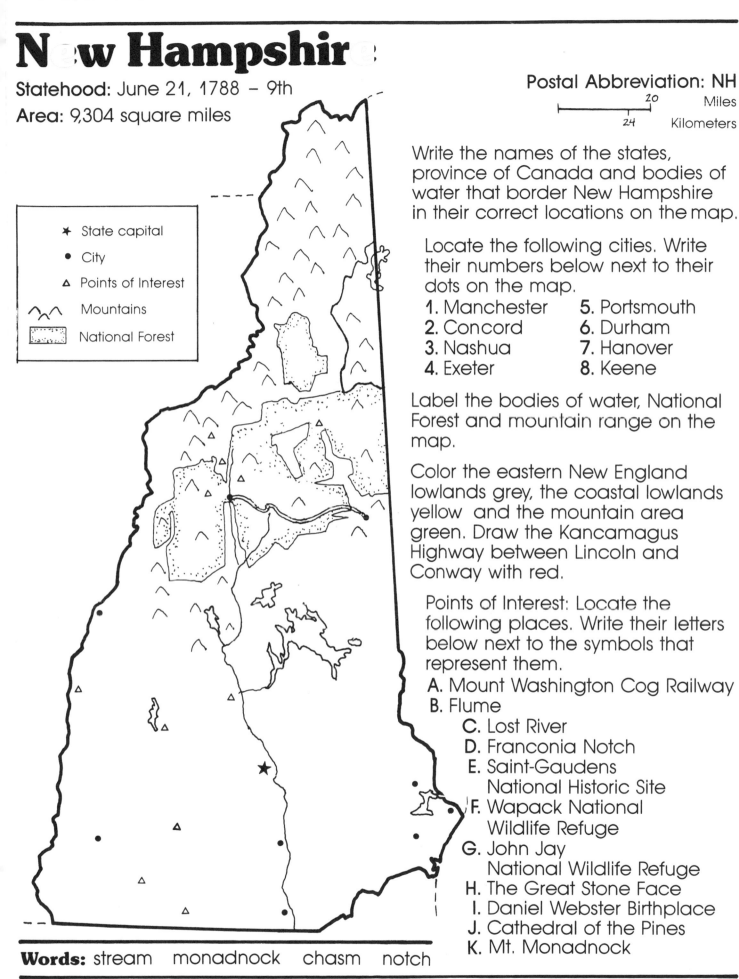

Legend
- ★ State capital
- • City
- △ Points of Interest
- ⌃⌃⌃ Mountains
- National Forest

Write the names of the states, province of Canada and bodies of water that border New Hampshire in their correct locations on the map.

Locate the following cities. Write their numbers below next to their dots on the map.

1. Manchester
2. Concord
3. Nashua
4. Exeter
5. Portsmouth
6. Durham
7. Hanover
8. Keene

Label the bodies of water, National Forest and mountain range on the map.

Color the eastern New England lowlands grey, the coastal lowlands yellow and the mountain area green. Draw the Kancamagus Highway between Lincoln and Conway with red.

Points of Interest: Locate the following places. Write their letters below next to the symbols that represent them.

A. Mount Washington Cog Railway
B. Flume
C. Lost River
D. Franconia Notch
E. Saint-Gaudens National Historic Site
F. Wapack National Wildlife Refuge
G. John Jay National Wildlife Refuge
H. The Great Stone Face
I. Daniel Webster Birthplace
J. Cathedral of the Pines
K. Mt. Monadnock

Words: stream   monadnock   chasm   notch

New Jersey

Statehood: December 18, 1787 – 3rd

Area: 7,836 square miles

Miles

Kilometers

Postal Abbreviation: NJ

★ State capital

• City

△ Points of Interest

⌃⌃ Mountains

⌐⌐ Plateaus

⌒⌒ Hills

Write the names of the states and bodies of water that border New Jersey in their correct locations on the map.

Locate the following cities. Write their numbers below next to their dots on the map.

1. Atlantic City
2. Camden
3. Trenton
4. Jersey City
5. Newark
6. Elizabeth
7. New Brunswick
8. Morristown
9. Hackettstown
10. Paterson
11. Vineland
12. Millville

The capital is _____.

Label the bodies of water and the Delaware Water Gap National Recreation Area on the map.

Color the Appalachian Ridge and Valley green, the New England uplands orange, the Piedmont Plateau brown and the Atlantic coastal plain grey.

Points of Interest: Locate the following places. Write their letters below next to the symbols that represent them.

A. Barnegat Lighthouse
B. Great Egg Harbor Inlet
C. Delaware Water Gap
D. Sandy Hook
E. Fort Dix
F. Birthplace of naval officer, James Lawrence, "Don't give up the ship."
G. High Point
H. Walt Whitman House
I. Princeton University
J. Seven Mile Boardwalk
K. Finns Point National Cemetery

Words:

hook   harbor   inlet

New Mexico

Statehood: January 6, 1912 – 47th

Area: 121,666 square miles

Postal Abbreviation: NM

60 Miles
80 Kilometers

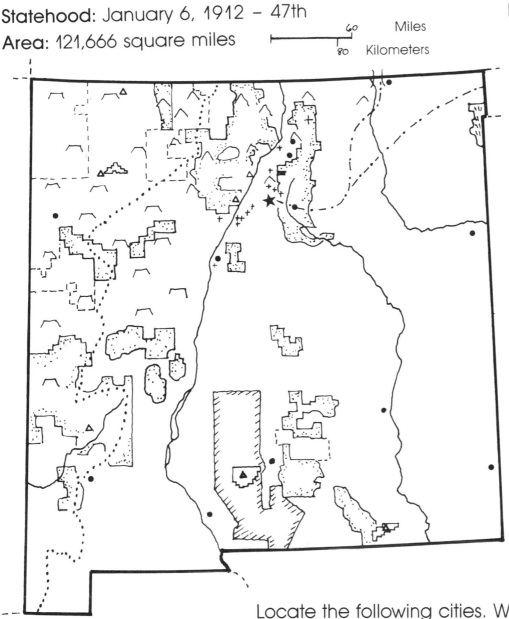

Legend:
- ★ State capital
- • City
- △ Points of Interest
- ⌒⌒ Mountains
- ⌒ Plateaus
- National Forest
- National Grassland
- Indian Reservations
- + Pueblos
- ⋯ Continental Divide
- —·— Santa Fe Trail

Write the names of the states and country that border New Mexico in their correct locations on the map.

Label the bodies of water, the National Forests and Grassland, the military range and the Navajo, Zuni, and Apache Indian Reservations.

Circle the Indian Pueblos. Trace over the Santa Fe Trail with red and the Continental Divide with blue.

Locate the following cities. Write their numbers below next to their dots on the map.

1. Albuquerque
2. Santa Fe
3. Arroyo Hondo
4. Alamogordo
5. Taos
6. Raton
7. Las Vegas
8. Gallup
9. Las Crucas
10. Silver City
11. Roswell
12. Hobbs
13. Tucumcari

Points of Interest: Locate the following places. Write their letters below next to the symbols that represent them.

A. Aztec Ruins National Monument
B. Chaco Canyon National Monument
C. Bandelier National Monument
D. Los Alamos Museum
E. White Sands National Monument
F. Gila Wilderness
G. Carlsbad Caverns National Monument

Words: arroyo   rio   pueblo   grassland

New York

Statehood: July 26, 1788 – 11th

Area: 49,576 square miles

40 Miles
60 Kilometers

Postal Abbreviation: NY

Write the names of the states, provinces of Canada and bodies of water that border New York in their correct locations on the map.

★ State capital
• City
△ Points of Interest
ᴧᴧ Mountains
⌢⌢ Plateaus

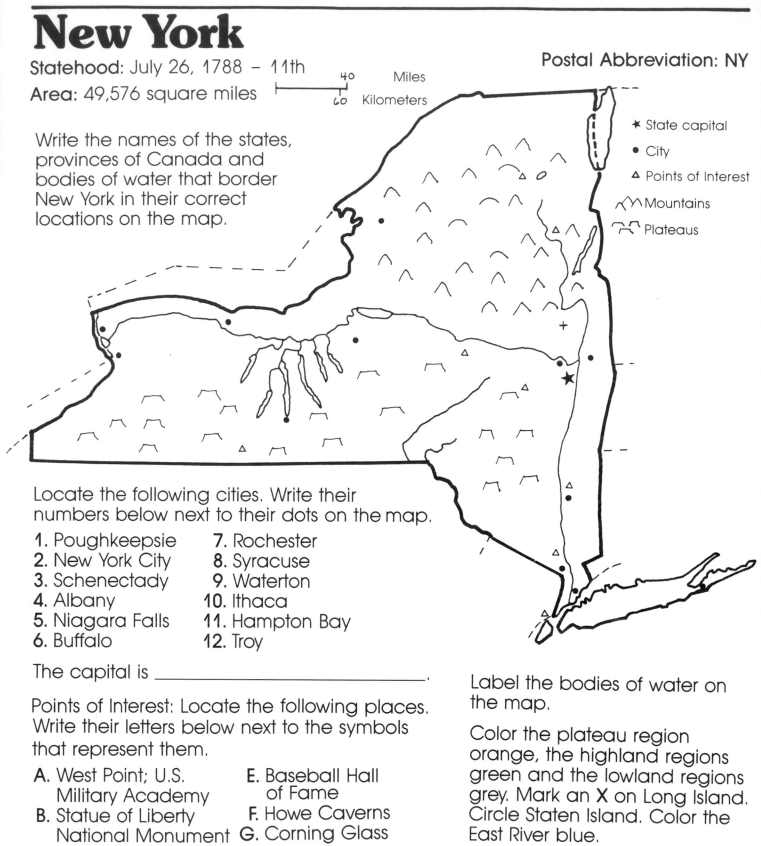

Locate the following cities. Write their numbers below next to their dots on the map.

1. Poughkeepsie
2. New York City
3. Schenectady
4. Albany
5. Niagara Falls
6. Buffalo
7. Rochester
8. Syracuse
9. Waterton
10. Ithaca
11. Hampton Bay
12. Troy

The capital is _____.

Points of Interest: Locate the following places. Write their letters below next to the symbols that represent them.

A. West Point; U.S. Military Academy
B. Statue of Liberty National Monument
C. Home of Franklin Delano Roosevelt National Historic Site
D. Fort Ticonderoga
E. Baseball Hall of Fame
F. Howe Caverns
G. Corning Glass Center
H. Robert Louis Stevenson Cottage

Label the bodies of water on the map.

Color the plateau region orange, the highland regions green and the lowland regions grey. Mark an **X** on Long Island. Circle Staten Island. Color the East River blue.

Words: canal   sound   island   urban

North Carolina

Statehood: November 21, 1789 – 12th
Area: 52,586 square miles

Postal Abbreviation: NC

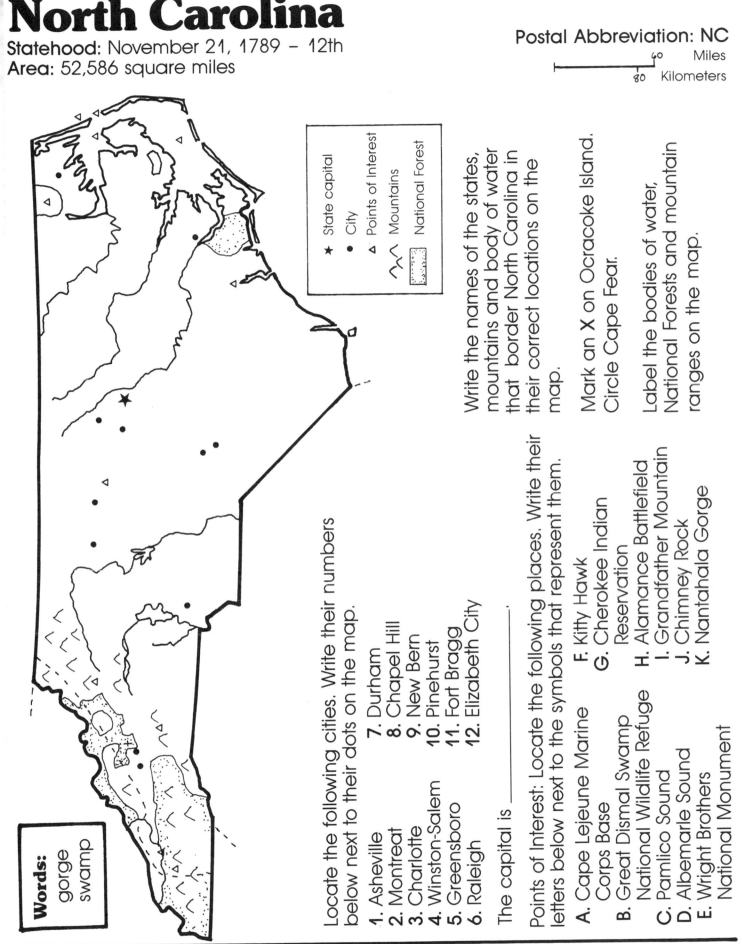

State capital
City
Points of Interest
Mountains
National Forest

Words:
gorge
swamp

Write the names of the states, mountains and body of water that border North Carolina in their correct locations on the map.

Mark an X on Ocracoke Island. Circle Cape Fear.

Label the bodies of water, National Forests and mountain ranges on the map.

Locate the following cities. Write their numbers below next to their dots on the map.

1. Asheville
2. Montreat
3. Charlotte
4. Winston-Salem
5. Greensboro
6. Raleigh
7. Durham
8. Chapel Hill
9. New Bern
10. Pinehurst
11. Fort Bragg
12. Elizabeth City

The capital is _____.

Points of Interest: Locate the following places. Write their letters below next to the symbols that represent them.

A. Cape Lejeune Marine Corps Base
B. Great Dismal Swamp National Wildlife Refuge
C. Pamlico Sound
D. Albemarle Sound
E. Wright Brothers National Monument
F. Kitty Hawk
G. Cherokee Indian Reservation
H. Alamance Battlefield
I. Grandfather Mountain
J. Chimney Rock
K. Nantahala Gorge

© 1990 Instructional Fair, Inc.

North Dakota

Statehood: November 2, 1889 – 39th

Area: 70,665 square miles

Postal Abbreviation: ND

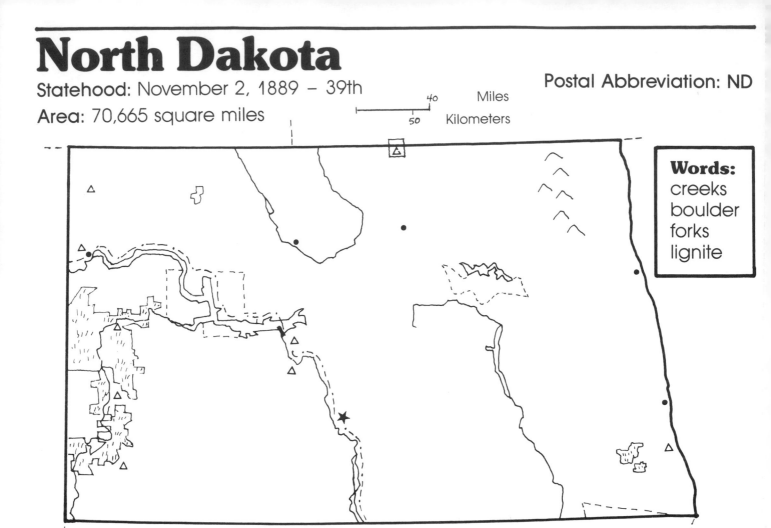

Words:
creeks
boulder
forks
lignite

★ State capital
● City
△ Points of Interest
⋀⋁ Mountains
National Grassland
Indian Reservations
Lewis and Clark Expedition

Label the bodies of water, National Grasslands and the mountains on the map.

Color the Indian reservations brown. Trace over the Lewis and Clark Expedition with brown. Circle Garrison Dam.

Write the names of the states, provinces of Canada and body of water that border North Dakota in their correct locations on the map.

Locate the following cities. Write their numbers below next to their dots on the map.

1. Bismark   **3.** Minot   **5.** Grand Forks
2. Williston   **4.** Rugby   **6.** Fargo

The capital is _____.

Points of Interest: Locate the following places. Write their letters below next to the symbols that represent them.

A. Theodore Roosevelt National Park
B. Fort Union Trading Post National Historic Site
C. Chateau De Mores Historic Site
D. Fort Mandan Historic Site
E. Knife River Indian Villages National Historic Site
F. Burning Lignite Beds
G. International Peace Gardens
H. Writing Rock
I. Fort Abercrombie

Ohio

Statehood: March 1, 1803 – 17th
Area: 41,222 square miles

Postal Abbreviation: OH

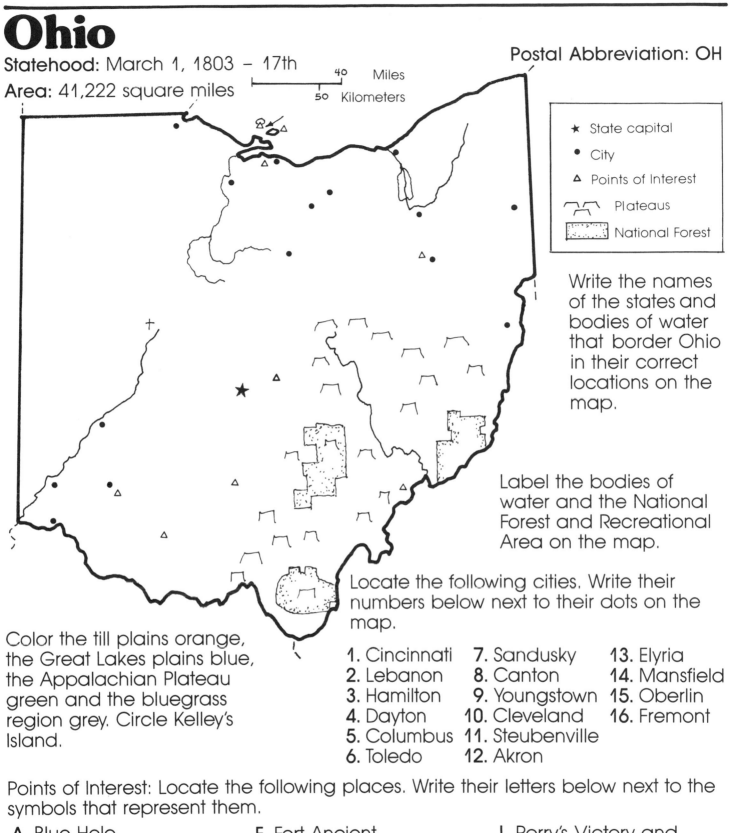

Write the names of the states and bodies of water that border Ohio in their correct locations on the map.

Label the bodies of water and the National Forest and Recreational Area on the map.

Color the till plains orange, the Great Lakes plains blue, the Appalachian Plateau green and the bluegrass region grey. Circle Kelley's Island.

Locate the following cities. Write their numbers below next to their dots on the map.

1. Cincinnati   7. Sandusky   13. Elyria
2. Lebanon   8. Canton   14. Mansfield
3. Hamilton   9. Youngstown   15. Oberlin
4. Dayton   10. Cleveland   16. Fremont
5. Columbus   11. Steubenville
6. Toledo   12. Akron

Points of Interest: Locate the following places. Write their letters below next to the symbols that represent them.

A. Blue Hole
B. Inscription Rock
C. Football Hall of Fame
D. Campus Martius Museum

E. Fort Ancient
F. Great Serpent Mound
G. Newark Earth Works
H. Mound City Group National Monument

I. Perry's Victory and International Peace Memorial

Words: valley   mound   bluegrass   till   grove

35   © 1990 Instructional Fair, Inc.

Oklahoma

Statehood: November 16, 1907 – 46th

Area: 69,919 square miles

Postal Abbreviation: OK

50 Miles
60 Kilometers

Trace over the Chisholm Trail with black. Color the gypsum hills brown, the sandstone hills red, the prairie plains green and the Ozark Plateau orange.

Points of Interest: Locate the following places. Write their letters below next to the symbols that represent them.

A. Washita Battlefield
B. Creek Capital
C. National Cowboy Hall of Fame
D. Will Rogers Memorial
E. Fort Sill Military Reservation and National Historic Landmark
F. Tsa-la-gi Indian Village

Legend:
- ★ State capital
- • City
- △ Points of Interest
- ∧∧ Mountains
- ⌒⌒ Plateaus
- ⌒ Hills
- National Forest
- National Grassland
- Chisholm Trail

Write the names of the states and bodies of water that border Oklahoma in their correct locations on the map.

Locate the following cities. Write their numbers below next to their dots on the map.

1. Oklahoma City
2. Tulsa
3. Norman
4. Anadarko
5. Lawton
6. Elk City
7. Miami
8. Claremore
9. Talequah
10. Muskogee

The capital is _____.

Label the bodies of water, mountains and National Forest and Grassland on the map.

Words: gypsum sandstone prairie

Oregon

Statehood: December 14, 1859 – 33rd
Area: 96,981 square miles

Postal Abbreviation: OR

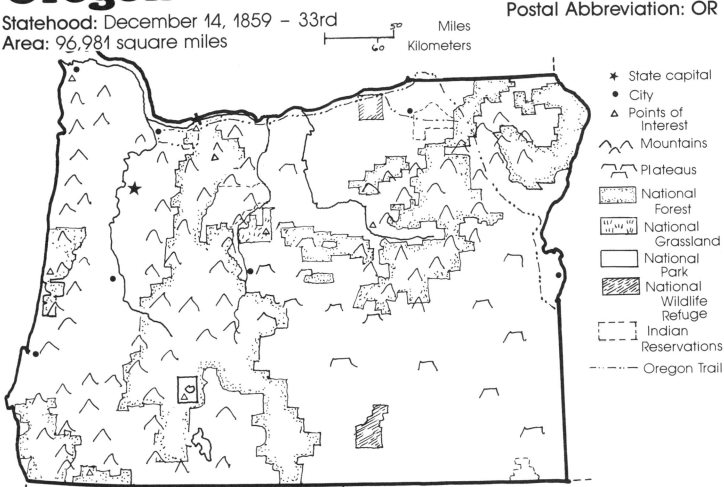

Miles
Kilometers

Legend:
- ✱ State capital
- • City
- △ Points of Interest
- ⋏⋏ Mountains
- ⋏⋏ Plateaus
- National Forest
- National Grassland
- National Park
- National Wildlife Refuge
- Indian Reservations
- Oregon Trail

Write the names of the states and the bodies of water that border Oregon in their correct locations on the map.

Locate the following cities. Write their numbers below next to the dots on the map.

1. Portland
2. Salem
3. Eugene
4. Astoria
5. Ontario
6. Pendleton
7. Coos Bay
8. Bend

Label the bodies of water and mountains on the map.

Trace over the Oregon Trail with green. Color the Indian Reservations brown. Circle Hart Mountain National Antelope Refuge. Mark an **X** on the U.S. Bombing Range. Color the National Forests green.

Points of Interest: Locate the following places. Write their letters below next to the symbols that represent them on the map.

A. Mount Hood
B. Crater Lake National Park
C. Oregon Caves National Monument
D. Fort Clatsop National Memorial
E. Sea Lions Cave
F. John Day Fossil Park
G. Columbia River Gorge/ Bonneville Dam
H. Crooked River National Grassland

Words: crater   beds

37

Pennsylvania

Statehood: December 12, 1787 – 2nd
Area: 45,333 square miles

Postal Abbreviation: PA

30 Miles
40 Kilometers

Legend

★ State capital
● City
△ Points of Interest
⌒ Mountains
⌐⌐ Plateaus
▢ National Forest

Label the bodies of water, the National Forest, two plateaus and two mountain ranges on the map.

Mark an X on the National Recreation Area. Color the Great Valley orange.

Words:

roadside   knob   burg

Write the names of the states and bodies of water that border Pennsylvania in their correct locations on the map.

Locate the following cities. Write their numbers below next to their dots on the map.

1. Philadelphia	5. Scranton	9. Pittsburgh
2. Allentown	6. Wilkes-Barre	10. Titusville
3. Bethlehem	7. Wellsboro	11. Erie
4. Reading	8. Gettysburg	12. Harrisburg

Points of Interest: Locate the following places. Write their letters below next to the symbols that represent them.

A. Valley Forge National Historic Park
B. Gettysburg National Military Park
C. Roadside America
D. Pine Creek Gorge
E. Rockville Bridge

F. Fort Necessity National Battlefield
G. Flagship Niagara
H. The Knobs
I. Hawk Mountain Sanctuary
J. Pennsylvania Farm Museum

Rhode Island

Statehood: May 29, 1790 – 13th

Area: 1,210 square miles

Miles

Kilometers

Postal Abbreviation: RI

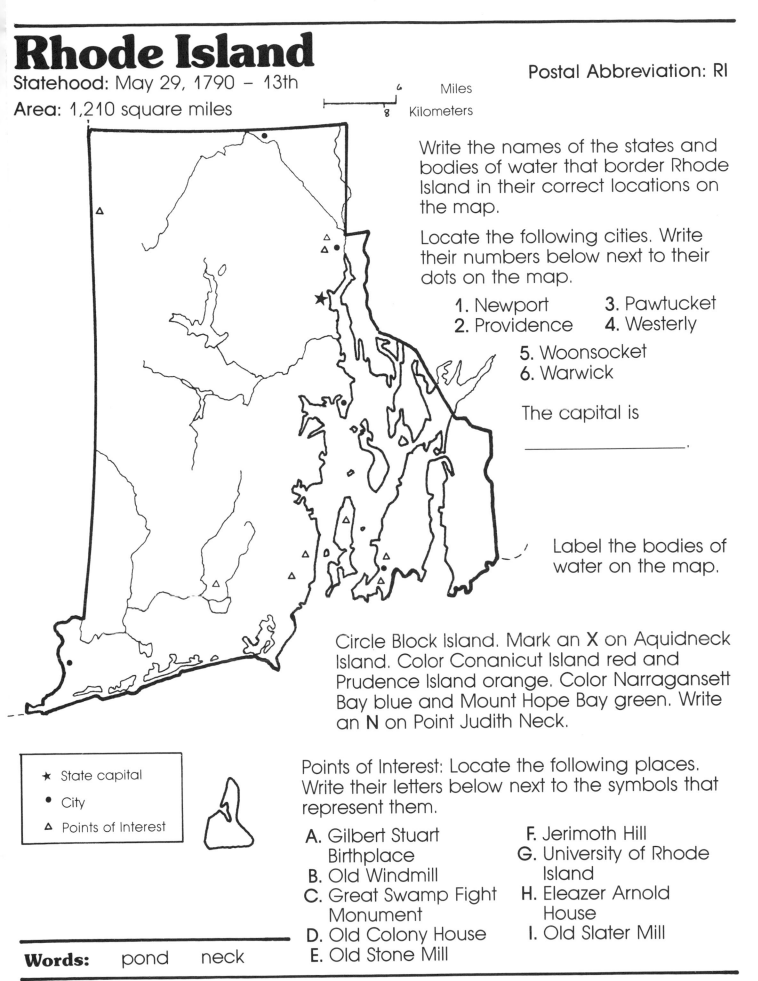

Write the names of the states and bodies of water that border Rhode Island in their correct locations on the map.

Locate the following cities. Write their numbers below next to their dots on the map.

1. Newport   3. Pawtucket
2. Providence 4. Westerly
               5. Woonsocket
               6. Warwick

The capital is

_____

Label the bodies of water on the map.

Circle Block Island. Mark an **X** on Aquidneck Island. Color Conanicut Island red and Prudence Island orange. Color Narragansett Bay blue and Mount Hope Bay green. Write an **N** on Point Judith Neck.

★ State capital

• City

△ Points of Interest

Points of Interest: Locate the following places. Write their letters below next to the symbols that represent them.

A. Gilbert Stuart Birthplace
B. Old Windmill
C. Great Swamp Fight Monument
D. Old Colony House
E. Old Stone Mill

F. Jerimoth Hill
G. University of Rhode Island
H. Eleazer Arnold House
I. Old Slater Mill

Words: pond   neck

South Carolina

Statehood: May 23, 1788 – 8th
Area: 31,055 square miles

40 Miles
50 Kilometers

Postal Abbreviation: SC

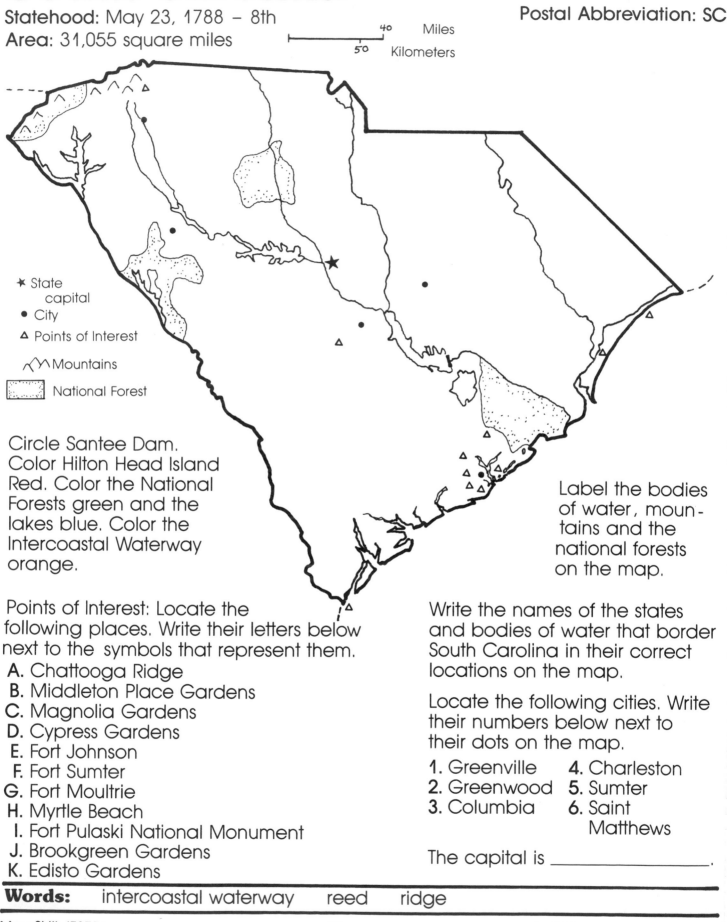

★ State capital
• City
△ Points of Interest
⌢⋀ Mountains
National Forest

Circle Santee Dam.
Color Hilton Head Island
Red. Color the National
Forests green and the
lakes blue. Color the
Intercoastal Waterway
orange.

Points of Interest: Locate the
following places. Write their letters below
next to the symbols that represent them.
A. Chattooga Ridge
B. Middleton Place Gardens
C. Magnolia Gardens
D. Cypress Gardens
E. Fort Johnson
F. Fort Sumter
G. Fort Moultrie
H. Myrtle Beach
I. Fort Pulaski National Monument
J. Brookgreen Gardens
K. Edisto Gardens

Label the bodies
of water, moun-
tains and the
national forests
on the map.

Write the names of the states
and bodies of water that border
South Carolina in their correct
locations on the map.

Locate the following cities. Write
their numbers below next to
their dots on the map.

1. Greenville   4. Charleston
2. Greenwood   5. Sumter
3. Columbia   6. Saint
                              Matthews

The capital is _____.

Words: intercoastal waterway   reed   ridge

South Dakota

Name_____

Statehood: November 2, 1889 – 40th

Area: 77,047 square miles

Postal Abbreviation: SD

40 Miles

50 Kilometers

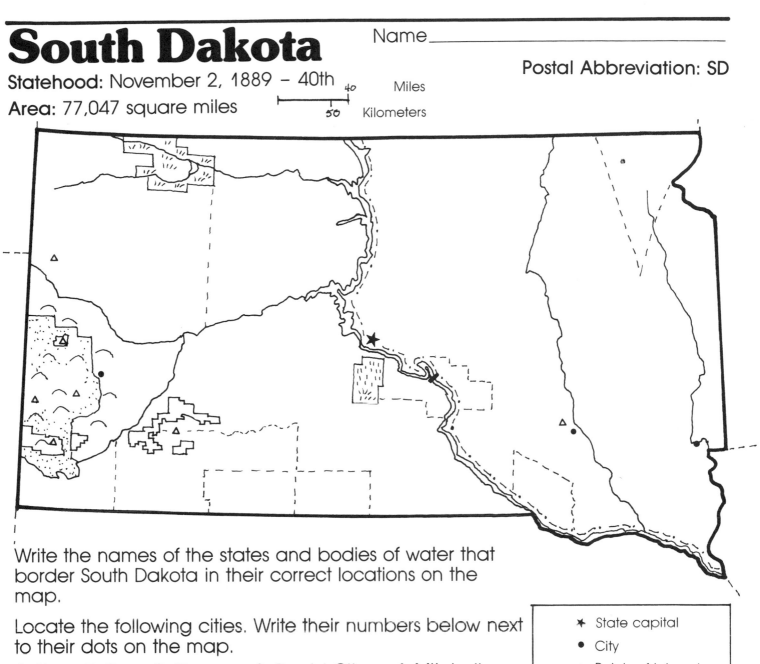

Write the names of the states and bodies of water that border South Dakota in their correct locations on the map.

Locate the following cities. Write their numbers below next to their dots on the map.

1. Sioux Falls   **2.** Pierre   **3.** Rapid City   **4.** Mitchell

Color the Indian Reservations brown. Trace over the Lewis and Clark Expedition with brown. Circle Big Bend Dam. Mark an **X** on the Great Lakes of South Dakota.

Points of Interest: Locate the following places. Write their letters below next to the symbols that represent them.

A. Badlands National Park
B. Jewel Cave National Monument
C. Mount Rushmore National Memorial
D. Geographic Center of the United States
E. Corn Palace
F. Deadwood
G. Fossil Cycad National Monument

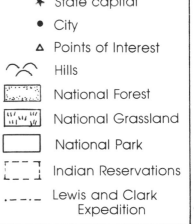

✶	State capital
●	City
△	Points of Interest
⌒⌒	Hills
[⋯]	National Forest
[ⅢⅢ]	National Grassland
[ ]	National Park
[- - -]	Indian Reservations
.—..—	Lewis and Clark Expedition

Label the bodies of water, the National Grasslands and the National Forest on the map.

Words: peak   cycad   badlands   traverse

Tennessee

Name _____

Statehood: June 1, 1796 – 16th

Area: 42,114 square miles

Postal Abbreviation: TN

50 Miles
60 Kilometers

Legend:
★ State capital
• City
△ Points of Interest
∧∧ Mountains
∿∿ Plateaus
▨ National Forest

Label the bodies of water, the mountain range and the National Forest on the map.

Words:
ridge   basin
cave   cavern

The capital is _____

Write the names of the states and bodies of water that border Tennessee in their correct locations on the map.

Locate the following cities. Write their numbers below next to their dots on the map.

1. Nashville
2. Knoxville
3. Memphis
4. Gatlinburg
5. Oak Ridge
6. Chattanooga
7. Smyrna
8. Spring Hill
9. Murfreesboro

Color the Cumberland Plateau yellow and the Great Valley green. Mark an X on Great Smoky Mountains National Park. Color the Nashville Basin blue. Draw a red line on the western highland rim and an orange line on the eastern highland rim.

Points of Interest: Locate the following places. Write their letters below next to the symbols that represent them.

A. U.S. Atomic Energy Commission
B. The Hermitage
C. Andrew Johnson National Historic Site
D. Jewel Cave
E. Clingman's Dome
F. Lookout Mountain Caverns
G. Railroad Museum
H. Palace Caverns
I. Indian Cave

Texas

Statehood: December 29, 1845 – 28th
Area: 266,807 square miles

Postal Abbreviation: TX

120 Miles
160 Kilometers

★ State capital
● City
△ Points of Interest
^^^ Mountains
National Forest
National Park
- - - - - Chisholm Trail

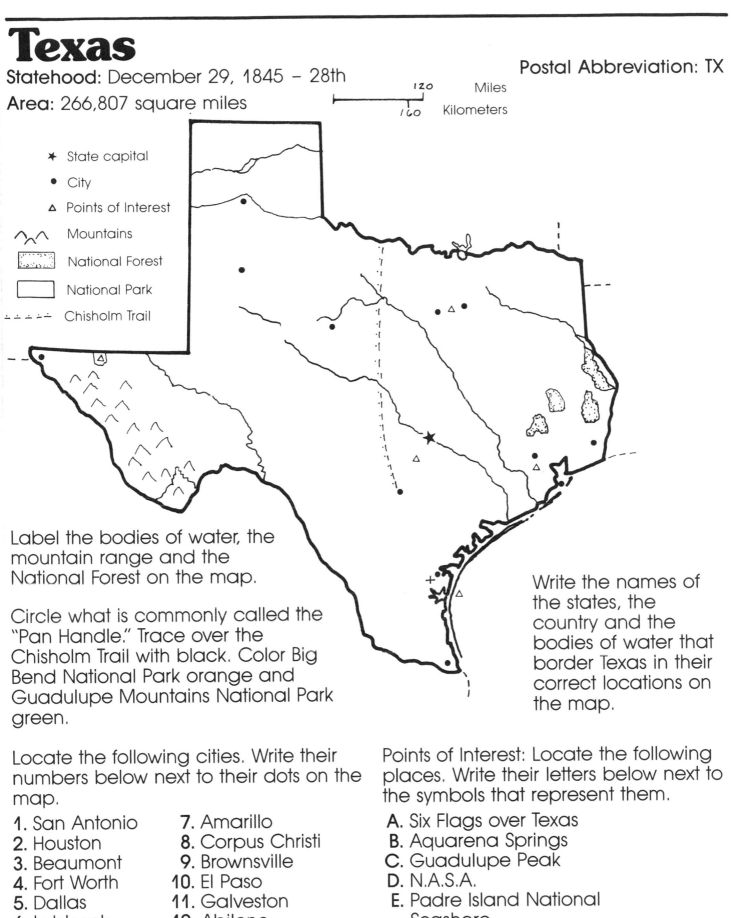

Label the bodies of water, the mountain range and the National Forest on the map.

Circle what is commonly called the "Pan Handle." Trace over the Chisholm Trail with black. Color Big Bend National Park orange and Guadulupe Mountains National Park green.

Write the names of the states, the country and the bodies of water that border Texas in their correct locations on the map.

Locate the following cities. Write their numbers below next to their dots on the map.

1. San Antonio
2. Houston
3. Beaumont
4. Fort Worth
5. Dallas
6. Lubbock
7. Amarillo
8. Corpus Christi
9. Brownsville
10. El Paso
11. Galveston
12. Abilene

The capital is _____.

Points of Interest: Locate the following places. Write their letters below next to the symbols that represent them.

A. Six Flags over Texas
B. Aquarena Springs
C. Guadulupe Peak
D. N.A.S.A.
E. Padre Island National Seashore

Words: seashore   trail

Utah

Statehood: January 4, 1896 – 45th
Area: 84,899 square miles

Postal Abbreviation: UT

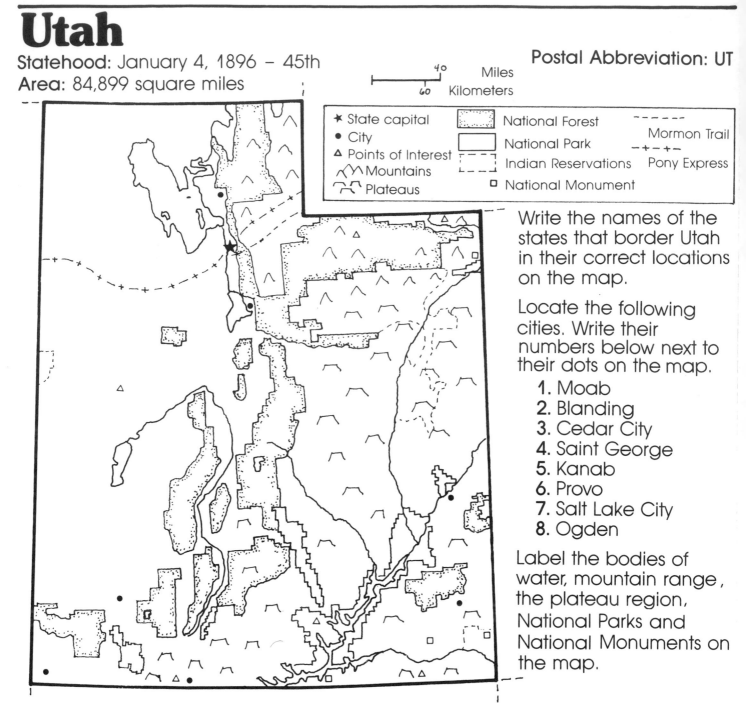

Scale: 40 Miles / 60 Kilometers

Legend:
- ★ State capital
- ● City
- △ Points of Interest
- ⋀⋁ Mountains
- ⌒ Plateaus
- National Forest
- National Park
- Indian Reservations
- ▫ National Monument
- – – – Mormon Trail
- –+–+– Pony Express

Write the names of the states that border Utah in their correct locations on the map.

Locate the following cities. Write their numbers below next to their dots on the map.

1. Moab
2. Blanding
3. Cedar City
4. Saint George
5. Kanab
6. Provo
7. Salt Lake City
8. Ogden

Label the bodies of water, mountain range, the plateau region, National Parks and National Monuments on the map.

Trace over the Pony Express with orange and the Mormon Trail with purple. Color the Cache National Forest blue, the Wasatch National Forest red, the Ashley National Forest grey, the Unita National Forest white, the Manti-la Sal National Forest orange, the Fishlake National Forest green and the Dixie National Forest purple. Color the Indian Reservation brown. Circle what is commonly called the "Four Corners" area.

Points of Interest: Locate the following places. Write their letters below next to the symbols that represent them.

A. Glen Canyon National Recreation Area
B. Monument Valley
C. Indian Cliff Ruins
D. Flaming Gorge National Recreation Area
E. Kings Peak
F. Sevier Desert

Words: arch   reef   cedar   bridge

Vermont

Name _____

Statehood: March 4, 1791 – 14th

Area: 9,614 square miles

Postal Abbreviation: VT

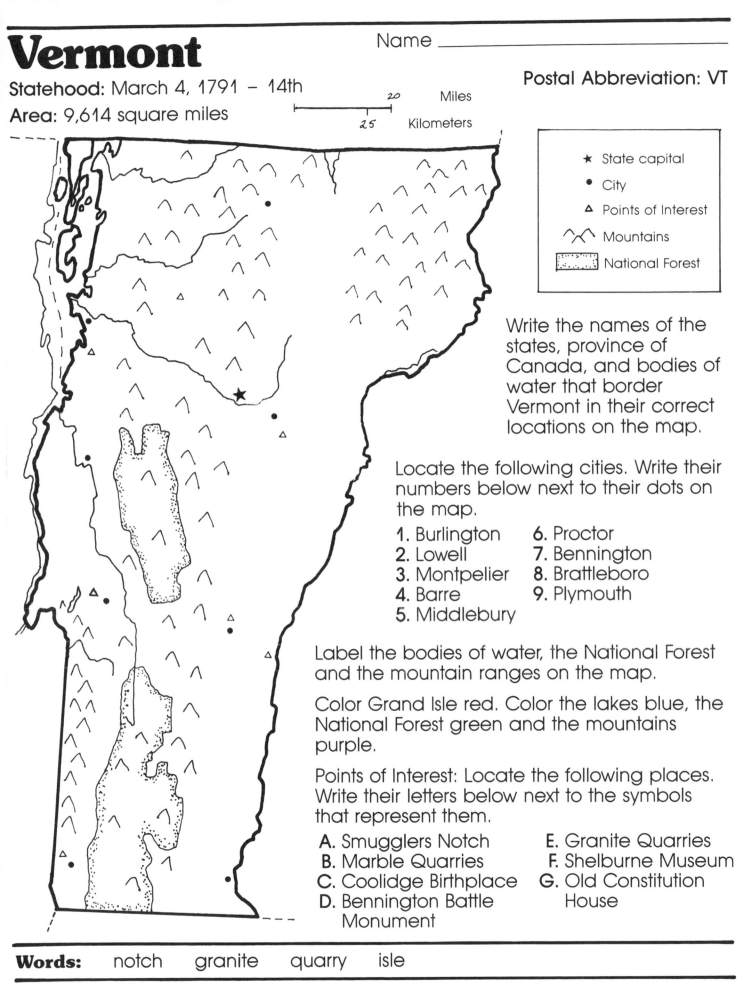

20 Miles

25 Kilometers

★ State capital
• City
△ Points of Interest
⌃⌃⌃ Mountains
[ ] National Forest

Write the names of the states, province of Canada, and bodies of water that border Vermont in their correct locations on the map.

Locate the following cities. Write their numbers below next to their dots on the map.

1. Burlington
2. Lowell
3. Montpelier
4. Barre
5. Middlebury
6. Proctor
7. Bennington
8. Brattleboro
9. Plymouth

Label the bodies of water, the National Forest and the mountain ranges on the map.

Color Grand Isle red. Color the lakes blue, the National Forest green and the mountains purple.

Points of Interest: Locate the following places. Write their letters below next to the symbols that represent them.

A. Smugglers Notch
B. Marble Quarries
C. Coolidge Birthplace
D. Bennington Battle Monument
E. Granite Quarries
F. Shelburne Museum
G. Old Constitution House

Words: notch   granite   quarry   isle

Virginia

Name_____

Statehood: June 25, 1788 – 10th

Area: 40,767 square miles

50 Miles
60 Kilometers

Postal Abbreviation: VA

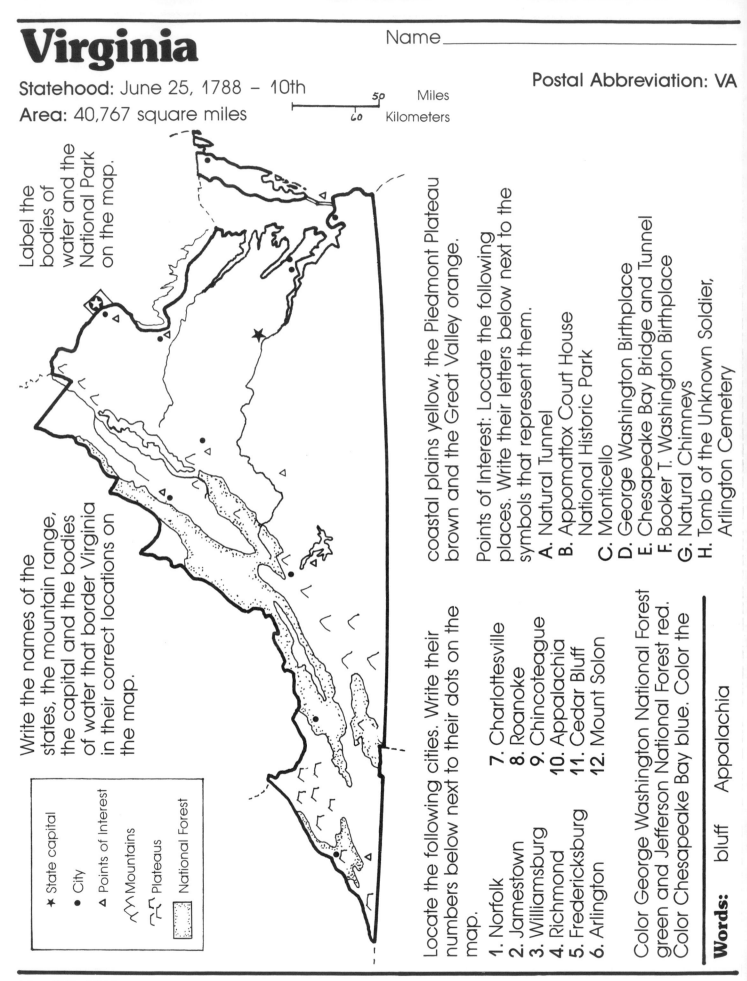

Label the bodies of water and the National Park on the map.

Write the names of the states, the mountain range, the capital and the bodies of water that border Virginia in their correct locations on the map.

Legend:
★ State capital
● City
▲ Points of Interest
⋀⋀ Mountains
⌐⌐ Plateaus
▦ National Forest

coastal plains yellow, the Piedmont Plateau brown and the Great Valley orange.

Points of Interest: Locate the following places. Write their letters below next to the symbols that represent them.

A. Natural Tunnel
B. Appomattox Court House National Historic Park
C. Monticello
D. George Washington Birthplace
E. Chesapeake Bay Bridge and Tunnel
F. Booker T. Washington Birthplace
G. Natural Chimneys
H. Tomb of the Unknown Soldier, Arlington Cemetery

Locate the following cities. Write their numbers below next to their dots on the map.

1. Norfolk
2. Jamestown
3. Williamsburg
4. Richmond
5. Fredericksburg
6. Arlington
7. Charlottesville
8. Roanoke
9. Chincoteague
10. Appalachia
11. Cedar Bluff
12. Mount Solon

Color George Washington National Forest green and Jefferson National Forest red. Color Chesapeake Bay blue. Color the

Words: bluff   Appalachia

Washington

Statehood: November 11, 1889 – 42nd

Area: 68,139 square miles

40 Miles
50 Kilometers

Postal Abbreviation: WA

Write the names of the states, bodies of water, and Canadian island and province that border Washington in their correct location on the map.

Locate the following cities. Write their numbers below next to their dots on the map.

1. Tacoma
2. Walla-Walla
3. Seattle
4. Spokane
5. Olympia
6. Port Angeles
7. Wenatchee
8. Aberdeen
9. Ilwaco

Trace the Lewis and Clark Expedition with brown. Color the National Forests green and the National Parks yellow. Color the Indian Reservations brown. Circle the dams.

Words: dam   port   coulee

★ State capital
● City
△ Points of Interest
⋀⋀ Mountains
⋀⋀ Plateaus

▒ National Forest
☐ National Park
⋮ Indian Reservations
– · – · Lewis and Clark Expedition

Label the bodies of water, the plateau and the mountain ranges on the map.

Points of Interest: Locate the following places. Write their letters below next to the symbols that represent them.

A. Mount Ranier
B. San Juan Islands
C. Ross Lake National Recreation Area
D. Grand Coulee Dam
E. Maryhill Museum
F. Fort Vancouver National Historic Site

West Virginia

Statehood: June 20, 1863 – 35th

Area: 24,231 square miles

Postal Abbreviation: WV

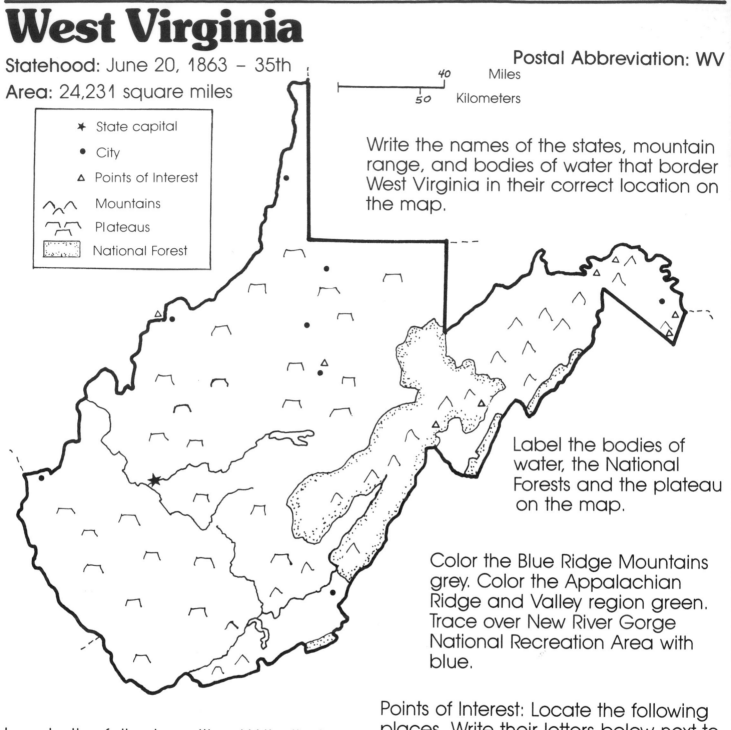

Legend:
- ★ State capital
- • City
- △ Points of Interest
- ∧∧ Mountains
- ⌒ Plateaus
- ▦ National Forest

Write the names of the states, mountain range, and bodies of water that border West Virginia in their correct location on the map.

Label the bodies of water, the National Forests and the plateau on the map.

Color the Blue Ridge Mountains grey. Color the Appalachian Ridge and Valley region green. Trace over New River Gorge National Recreation Area with blue.

Locate the following cities. Write their numbers below next to their dots on the map.

1. Huntington
2. Parkersburg
3. Wheeling
4. Charleston
5. White Sulphur Springs
6. Martinsburg
7. Weston
8. Clarksburg
9. Morgantown

Points of Interest: Locate the following places. Write their letters below next to the symbols that represent them.

A. Jacksons Mill
B. Seneca Rock
C. Cass Scenic Railroad
D. Blennerhassett Island
E. Harpers Ferry
F. Charles Town
G. Chesapeake and Ohio Canal National Historic Park
H. Berkely Springs

Words: sulphur   range   ferry

Wisconsin

Statehood: May 29, 1848 – 30th
Area: 56,153 square miles

Postal Abbreviation: WI

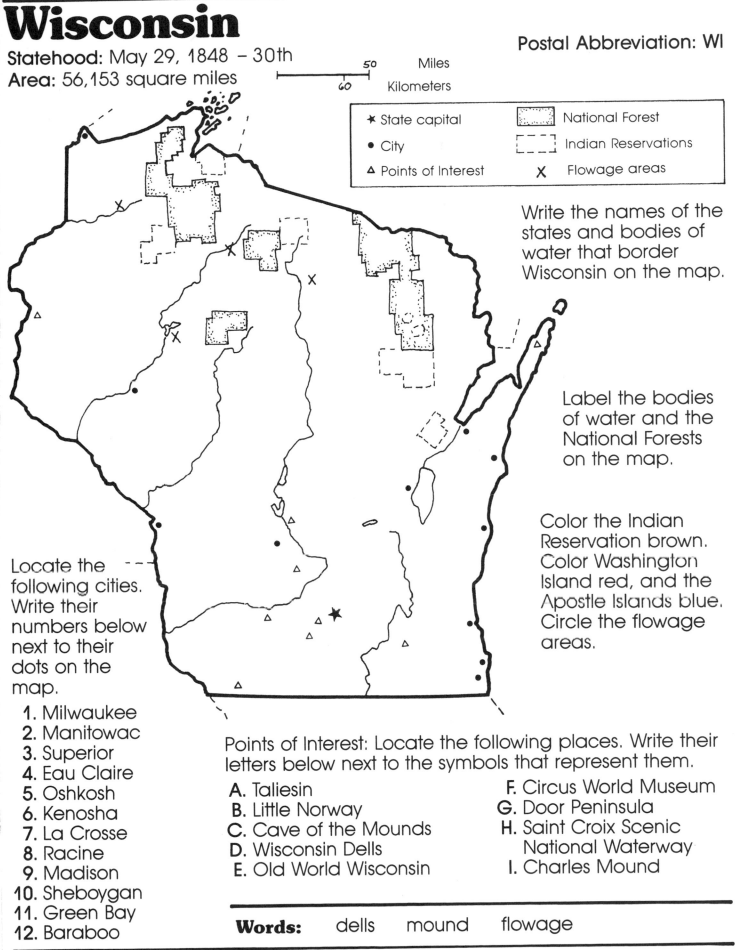

50 Miles
60 Kilometers

★ State capital
● City
△ Points of Interest

National Forest
Indian Reservations
✗ Flowage areas

Write the names of the states and bodies of water that border Wisconsin on the map.

Label the bodies of water and the National Forests on the map.

Color the Indian Reservation brown. Color Washington Island red, and the Apostle Islands blue. Circle the flowage areas.

Locate the following cities. Write their numbers below next to their dots on the map.

1. Milwaukee
2. Manitowac
3. Superior
4. Eau Claire
5. Oshkosh
6. Kenosha
7. La Crosse
8. Racine
9. Madison
10. Sheboygan
11. Green Bay
12. Baraboo

Points of Interest: Locate the following places. Write their letters below next to the symbols that represent them.

A. Taliesin
B. Little Norway
C. Cave of the Mounds
D. Wisconsin Dells
E. Old World Wisconsin

F. Circus World Museum
G. Door Peninsula
H. Saint Croix Scenic National Waterway
I. Charles Mound

Words: dells   mound   flowage

Wyoming

Statehood: July 10, 1890 – 44th

Area: 97,809 square miles

Postal Abbreviation: WY

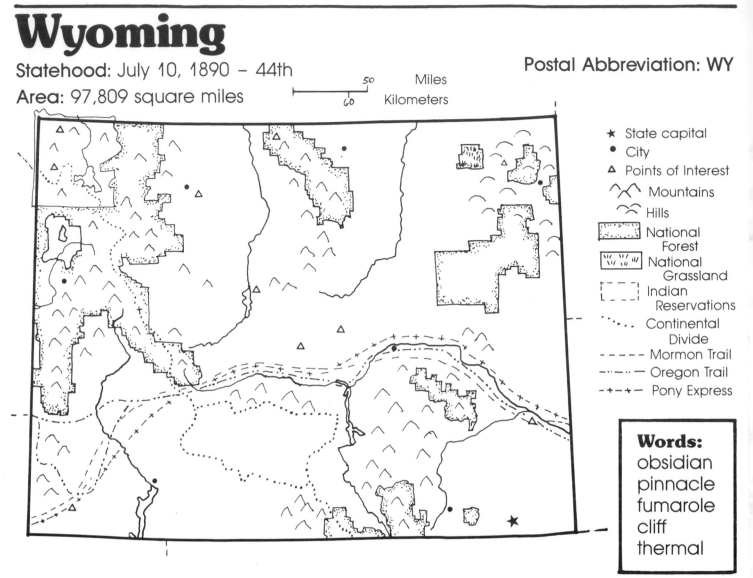

Legend:
- ★ State capital
- • City
- △ Points of Interest
- ⌃⌃⌃ Mountains
- ⌃⌃ Hills
- National Forest
- National Grassland
- Indian Reservations
- ⋯ Continental Divide
- – – – Mormon Trail
- –·–· Oregon Trail
- –+–+ Pony Express

Words:
obsidian
pinnacle
fumarole
cliff
thermal

Write the names of the states that border Wyoming in their correct location.

Locate the following cities. Write their numbers below next to their dots on the map.

1. Cheyenne   3. Casper   5. Sheridan   7. Jackson
2. Laramie   4. Sundance   6. Cody   8. Green River

Label the bodies of water, National Parks and Grasslands, and mountain ranges on the map.

Color the Indian Reservation brown. Trace over the Oregon Trail green, the Pony Express orange; the Mormon Trail red and the Continental Divide with blue. Color the National Forests green.

Points of Interest: Locate the following places. Write their letters below next to the symbols that represent them.

A. Spirit Mountain Cavern   E. Old Faithful Geyser   I. Castle Gardens Petroglyph Site
B. Medicine Wheel   F. Fort Bridger
C. Wind River Canyon   G. Hells Half Acre   J. Pinnacle Peaks
D. Hot Springs   H. Fort Laramie

World Locations and Facts

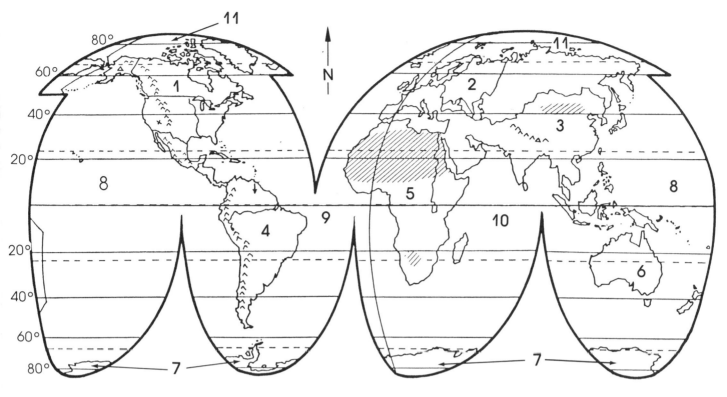

| ∧∧∧ Mountain Range | ⌒ Rivers | X Canyon |
| △ Mountain Peak | ▨ Desert | ↓ Waterfall |

Write the names of the continents and bodies of water on the map as indicated by the following numbers.

1. _____   4. _____   7. _____   10. _____
2. _____   5. _____   8. _____   11. _____
3. _____   6. _____   9. _____

Color the Equator green, Tropic of Cancer yellow, Tropic of Capricorn orange, Arctic Circle blue, Antarctic Circle red, Prime Meridian purple and the International Date Line brown.

Mark a blue X on the world's longest river and a green X on the world's highest mountain peak.

Circle the world's largest lake green, the world's largest island red, the world's highest mountain range black, the world's largest desert yellow and the world's largest peninsula orange.

Color the world's largest country brown.

What is the name of the world's largest canyon and where is it located?

_____ Highest peak and where is it located?

_____

Highest waterfall and where is it located? _____

Label all the rivers, lakes, peaks and deserts shown on the map.

Four Hemispheres

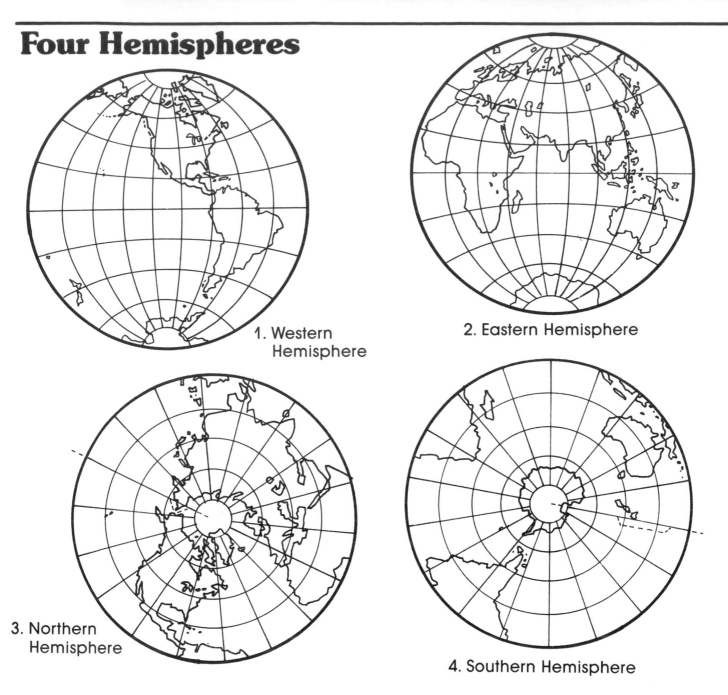

1. Western Hemisphere

2. Eastern Hemisphere

3. Northern Hemisphere

4. Southern Hemisphere

Match the numbers on these hemispheric maps with the names below. Most names will have more than one number.

_____ North America   _____ South America   _____ Australia

_____ Asia   _____ Africa   _____ Europe   _____ Antarctica

_____ Atlantic Ocean   _____ Pacific Ocean   _____ Indian Ocean

_____ Arctic Ocean   _____ Antarctic Ocean   _____ Equator

_____ Arctic Circle   _____ North Pole   _____ Tropic of Cancer

_____ Tropic of Capricorn   _____ Antarctic Circle   _____ Prime Meridian

_____ International Date Line

On another piece of paper define: Continent, Eurasia, Hemisphere, Prime Meridian, International Date Line.

The Western Hemisphere

The list below contains the names of geographic places in the Western Hemisphere. Match the names with their letter locations on the map.

___ Bering Sea
___ Beaufort Sea
___ Labrador Sea
___ Caribbean Sea
___ Gulf of Mexico
___ Bering Strait
___ Bermuda
___ Drake Passage
___ Gulf of Panama
___ Gulf of Alaska
___ Aleutian Islands
___ Hawaiian Islands
___ West Indies

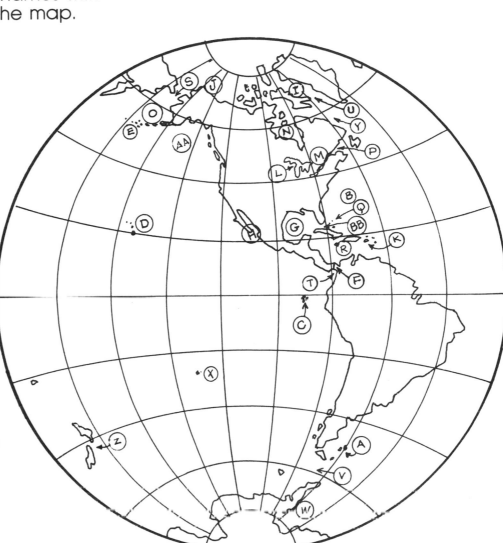

___ Gulf of St. Lawrence
___ Falkland Islands
___ Gulf of California
___ Weddell Sea
___ Great Lakes
___ Straits of Florida
___ Hudson Bay
___ Baffin Bay
___ Davis Strait
___ Panama Canal
___ Galapagos Islands
___ Bahamas
___ Easter Island
___ St. Lawrence Seaway
___ New Zealand

Island Hopping Trivia Match

___ Galapagos Island   1. Eric the Red
___ Kodiak Island   2. June 1942
___ Falkland Islands   3. Giant Tortoise
___ Greenland   4. U.S. Territory
___ Midway Island   5. Brown Bear
___ Puerto Rico   6. British/Argentine War
___ Easter Island   7. St. George Medical
        School
___ Grenada   8. Megaliths
___ Pitcairn Island   9. United Kingdom

The Eastern Hemisphere

The list below contains the names of geographic places in the Eastern Hemisphere. Match the names with their letter locations on the map

___ Greenland Sea
___ Norwegian Sea
___ Mediterranean Sea
___ Arabian Sea
___ South China Sea
___ East China Sea
___ Sea of Okhotsk
___ Caspian Sea
___ Black Sea
___ Red Sea
___ Aral Sea
___ Baltic Sea
___ North Sea
___ Tasman Sea
___ Persian Gulf
___ Bay of Bengal
___ Gulf of Thailand
___ English Channel
___ Strait of Gibralter
___ Barents Sea
___ Gulf of Aden
___ Yellow Sea
___ Sea of Japan
___ Mozambique Channel
___ Coral Sea
___ Kara Sea

BRAIN TEASER: Cross out the one term in each group that does not fit and tell why.

1. White, Red, Black, Coral, Blue _____

_____

2. Strait, Sound, Channel, Canal, Bay _____

_____

3. Tahiti, Tasmania, Guam, Madagascar, Auckland

_____

4. Baltic, Coral, Aral, Arabian, Kara _____

_____

SPECIAL MARKINGS: Make an **X** on the Suez Canal. Circle Lake Victoria. Draw a triangle around Madagascar.

The Northern Hemisphere

Write the numbers next to the cities listed below beside the dots representing their locations on the map.

1. New York
2. Madrid
3. Moscow
4. Bombay
5. Tokyo
6. Fairbanks
7. New Orleans
8. Paris
9. Rome
10. Calcutta
11. Hong Kong

12. Anchorage
13. Vancouver
14. Seattle
15. Chicago
16. Lisbon

17. London
18. Stockholm
19. Cairo
20. Tehran
21. Beijing

22. San Francisco
23. Mexico City
24. Montreal
25. Thule
26. Berlin
27. Oslo
28. Ankara
29. Shanghai
30. Los Angeles
31. Tripoli
32. Warsaw

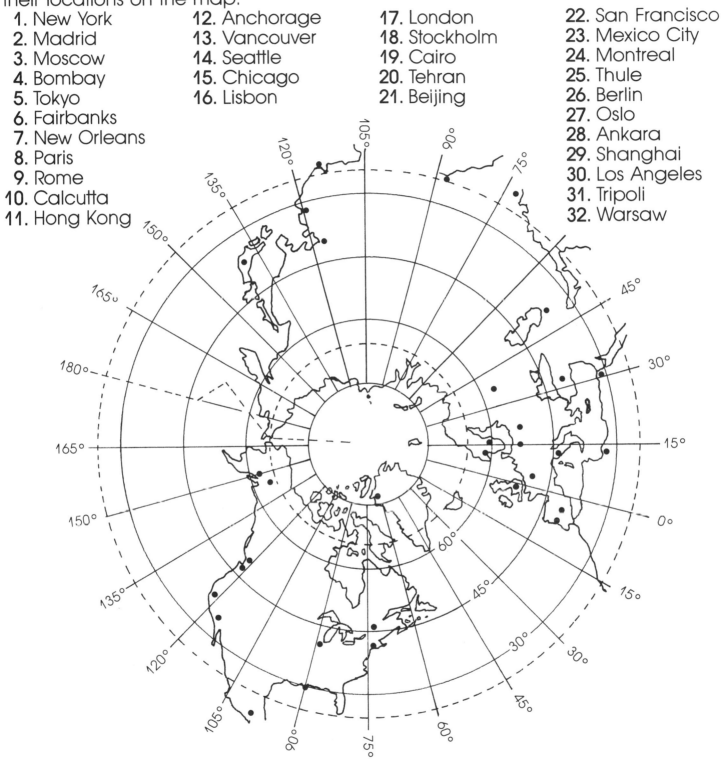

Name the continents in the Northern Hemisphere._____
Label the Pacific, Arctic and Atlantic Oceans. Circle the North Pole.
EXTRA CREDIT: On another piece of paper, write the names of the cities shown on the map and the name of the country in which each is located.

The Southern Hemisphere

The list below contains the names of geographic places in the Southern Hemisphere. Match the names with their letter locations on the map.

___ South America
___ Ronne Ice Shelf
___ Transantarctic Mountains
___ Tasmania

___ Port Elizabeth
___ Africa
___ Cape Town

___ British Antarctic Territory
___ International Date Line
___ Ross Ice Shelf
___ Australia
___ Australian Antarctic Territory
___ Ross Sea
___ Melbourne
___ South Pole
___ Chilean Claim
___ France's Claim
___ Cape Horn
___ Amundsen Sea
___ New Zealand's Claim
___ Antarctic Peninsula
___ Argentinian Claim
___ South Island
___ North Island

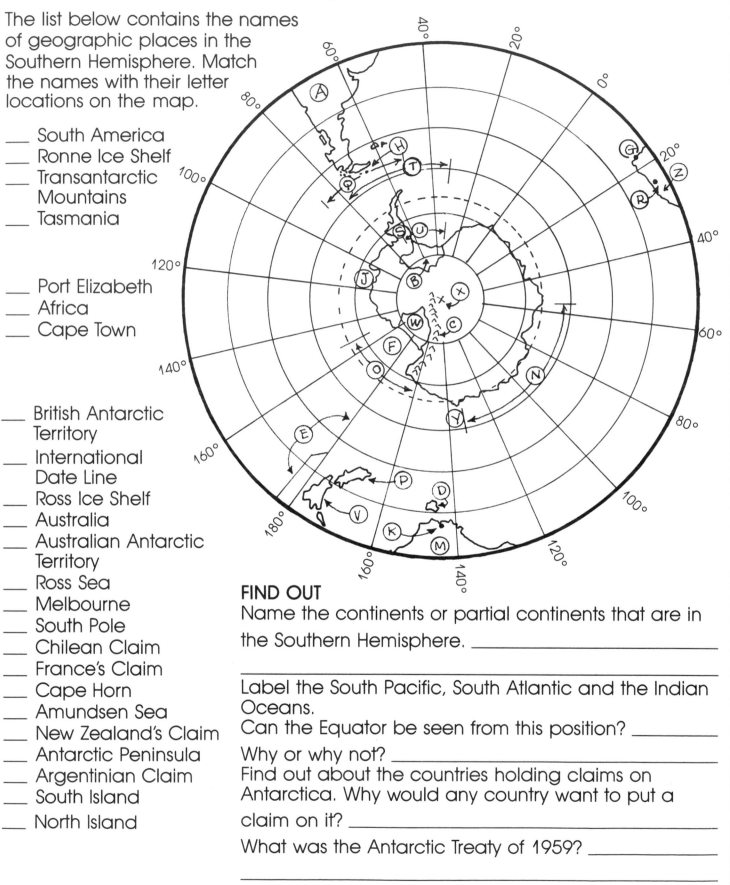

FIND OUT

Name the continents or partial continents that are in the Southern Hemisphere. _____

_____

Label the South Pacific, South Atlantic and the Indian Oceans.
Can the Equator be seen from this position? _____

Why or why not? _____

Find out about the countries holding claims on Antarctica. Why would any country want to put a claim on it? _____

What was the Antarctic Treaty of 1959? _____

_____

For whom is the Amundsen Sea named? _____

Australia

Area: 2,966,000 sq. mi. Greatest Distances:
   North-South 1950 mi.
   East-West 2475 mi.

Map Legend:
- ∧∧ ∧∧ Mountains
- ▨ Desert
- + Highest Point
- ⊖ Lowest Point
- ∿∿ Great Barrier Reef

500 miles
500 kilometers

Label the following bodies of water:
   Coral Sea
   Gulf of Carpentaria
   Great Australian Bight
   Tasman Sea
   Indian Ocean
   Arafura Sea
   Timor Sea
   Torres Strait
   Bass Strait

Color the states and territories of Australia as directed following each one's name.

Northern Territory (blue)
Western Australia (red)
South Australia (grey)
New South Wales (green)

Queensland (brown)
Victoria (orange)
Tasmania (purple)

Write the number of each desert below on the map to show where it is located.
   1. Great Sandy Desert
   2. Great Victoria Desert
   3. Gibson Desert
   4. Simpson Desert

Label the Great Barrier Reef.
Mark an **X** on the Great Dividing Range and circle Papua New Guinea.
What is the highest point in Australia? _____

What is the lowest? _____

Match the following Australian trivia and vocabulary.

A. Stations	**B.** Outback	**C.** Continent	**D.** Squatters	**E.** Buckjumpers
F. Down Under	**G.** Brumbies	**H.** Canberra	**I.** Aborigines	**J.** Mob

___ Geographic Reference   ___ Capital City   ___ Herd of Animals
___ Interior of Country   ___ First Residents   ___ Wild Horses
___ Country   ___ Ranches ___ Ranch Owners   ___ Bucking Broncos

Antarctica

Area: 5,100,000 sq. mi.

Greatest Linear Distance: 3250 mi.

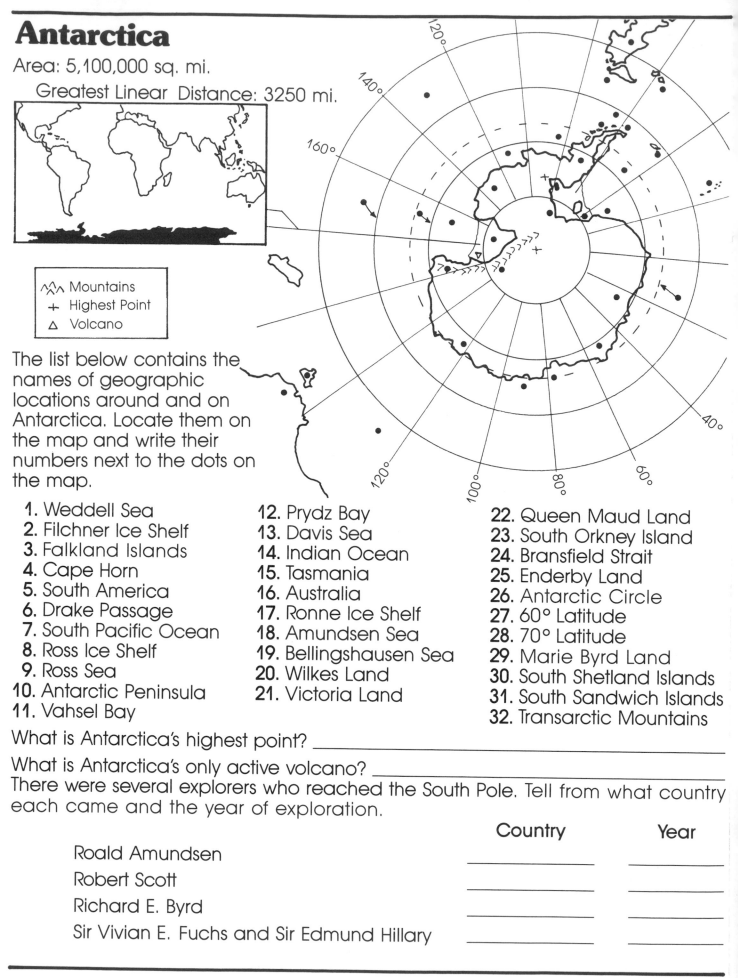

- ᴧᴧᴧ Mountains
- + Highest Point
- △ Volcano

The list below contains the names of geographic locations around and on Antarctica. Locate them on the map and write their numbers next to the dots on the map.

1. Weddell Sea
2. Filchner Ice Shelf
3. Falkland Islands
4. Cape Horn
5. South America
6. Drake Passage
7. South Pacific Ocean
8. Ross Ice Shelf
9. Ross Sea
10. Antarctic Peninsula
11. Vahsel Bay

12. Prydz Bay
13. Davis Sea
14. Indian Ocean
15. Tasmania
16. Australia
17. Ronne Ice Shelf
18. Amundsen Sea
19. Bellingshausen Sea
20. Wilkes Land
21. Victoria Land

22. Queen Maud Land
23. South Orkney Island
24. Bransfield Strait
25. Enderby Land
26. Antarctic Circle
27. 60° Latitude
28. 70° Latitude
29. Marie Byrd Land
30. South Shetland Islands
31. South Sandwich Islands
32. Transarctic Mountains

What is Antarctica's highest point? _____

What is Antarctica's only active volcano? _____

There were several explorers who reached the South Pole. Tell from what country each came and the year of exploration.

	Country	Year
Roald Amundsen	_____	_____
Robert Scott	_____	_____
Richard E. Byrd	_____	_____
Sir Vivian E. Fuchs and Sir Edmund Hillary	_____	_____

Canada

Area: 3,831,033 sq. mi.
Greatest Distances: North-South 2875 mi.
East-West 3223 mi.

Label the
mountains.

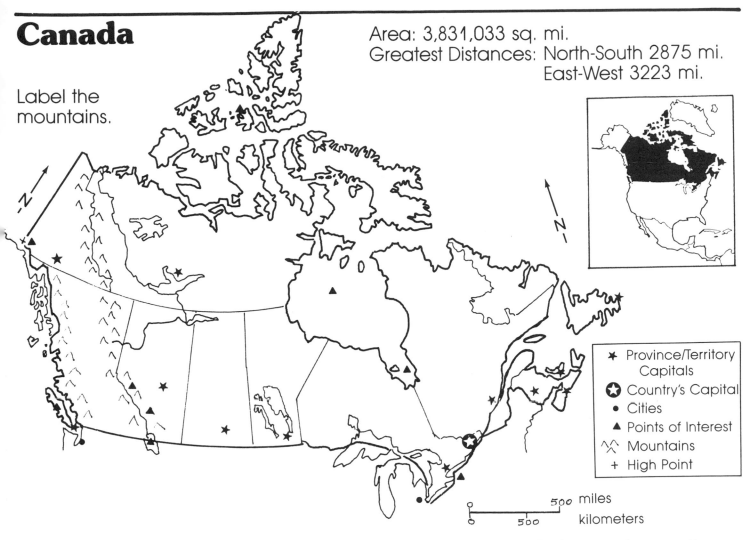

Legend:
✱ Province/Territory Capitals
★ Country's Capital
• Cities
▲ Points of Interest
⋀⋀ Mountains
+ High Point

500 miles
500 kilometers

Locate Canada's provinces and territories listed below. Color each one the color following its name in parenthesis.

Alberta (orange)	New Brunswick (green)	Nova Scotia (brown)
Quebec (yellow)	British Columbia (blue)	Newfoundland (red)
Ontario (green)	Saskatchewan (red)	Manitoba (brown)
Yukon (yellow)	Northwest Territories (blue)	Prince Edward Island (purple)

Locate each capital. Write the number next to the star in each province or territory where it belongs.

The country's capital is _____.

1. Edmonton	3. Fredericton	6. Halifax	8. Quebec	11. Victoria
2. St. Johns	4. Toronto	7. Regina	9. Winnipeg	12. Yellowknife
	5. Charlottetown		10. Whitehorse	

Trace with blue and label the Mackenzie-Peace and St. Lawrence Rivers. Locate the following Points of Interest. Write their letters below next to the symbols that represent them.

A. Hudson Bay	D. Banff	G. Magnetic North Pole
B. Vancouver Island	E. Jasper	H. Mt. Logan
C. Waterton-Glacier	F. Niagara Falls	I. James Bay
International Peace Park		

Which Great Lake is not part of Canada? _____

Locate Seattle and Detroit. Write the name in the proper locations.

The United States of America

Area: 3,618,770 sq. mi. Greatest Distances: North-South 1598 mi., East-West 2807 mi.

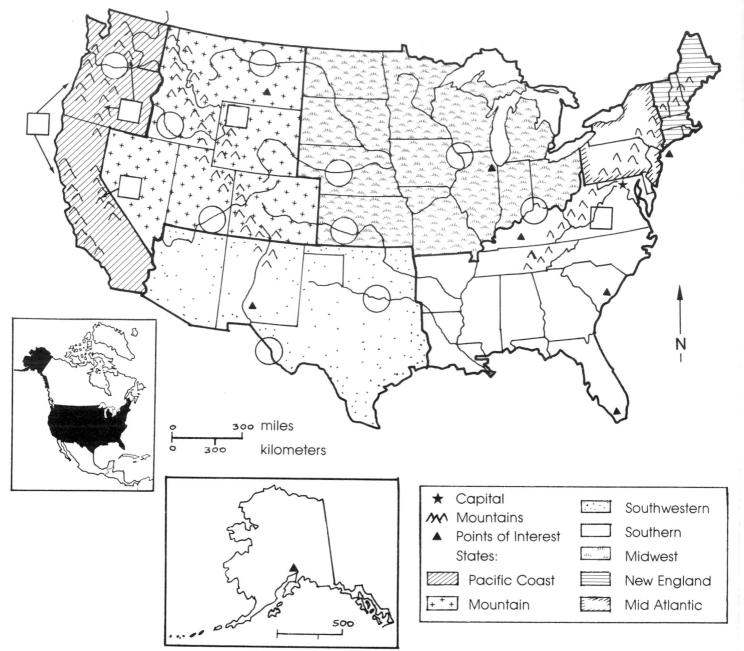

★ Capital
ᴧᴧ Mountains
▲ Points of Interest

States:
⧄ Pacific Coast
+ + + Mountain

∶∶∶ Southwestern
▭ Southern
⌁ Midwest
≡ New England
⧄ Mid Atlantic

The United States is divided into seven geographic regions where the climate, terrain and background are similar. List the regions and states in each.

_____   _____
_____   _____
_____   _____
_____   _____
_____   _____
                           _____

The United States (continued)

_____   _____
                _____
                _____
_____   _____
                _____
_____   _____

Color the Great Lakes blue and write their letters below on the map.
Trace over the rivers with blue and write their letters below in the correct ○ 's on the map. Color the mountain ranges purple and write their letters below in the correct □ 's on the map.

A. Lake Superior	H. Arkansas River	O. Columbia River
B. Lake Huron	I. Red River	P. Coastal Mountains
C. Lake Erie	J. Colorado River	Q. Rocky Mountains
D. Lake Michigan	K. Rio Grande River	R. Sierra Nevadas
E. Lake Ontario	L. Mississippi River	S. Appalachians
F. Ohio River	M. Snake River	T. Cascade Mountains
G. Missouri River	N. Platte River	

Which states touch Canadian soil? _____

_____

Which states touch Mexican soil? _____   _____

_____

Which state is not part of the North American continent? _____

What is the country's capital? _____

Locate the following Points of Interest. Write their numbers below next to the symbols that represent them.

1. Sears Tower	5. United Nations
2. Everglades National Park	6. Kenai Fjords
3. Mammoth Cave	7. Custer Battlefield
4. White Sands	8. Fort Sumter

Greenland

Area: 840,050 sq. mi.

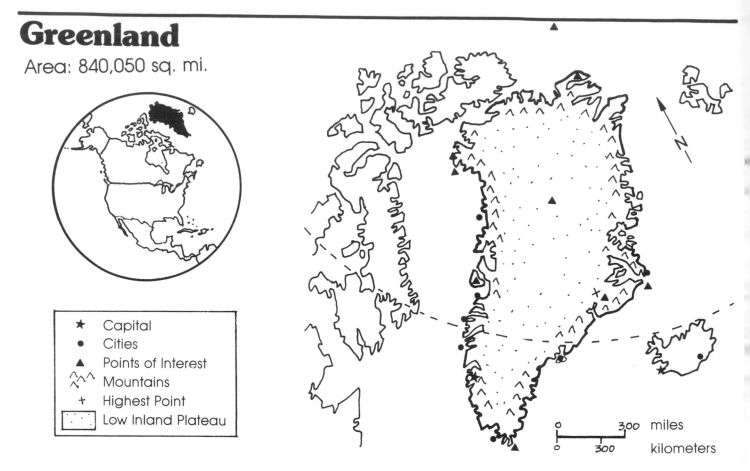

★ Capital
● Cities
▲ Points of Interest
⋀⋀⋀ Mountains
+ Highest Point
⋯ Low Inland Plateau

Color the Low Inland Plateau green and the coastal mountains orange. Color Canada purple, Svalbard red and Iceland blue.

To what country does Greenland belong? _____
Explain why Greenland is part of the North American continent even though the country to which it belongs is not.

_____

Circle the point on the map orange where Greenland is only ten miles from the North American Continent. Trace over the Arctic Circle with red.
Label the following bodies of water.

Denmark Strait	Labrador Sea	Lincoln Sea
Hudson Strait	Baffin Bay	North Atlantic Ocean
Greenland Sea	Davis Strait	

Locate the following cities. Write their letters next to the dots representing them on the map.

A. Egedesminde   **C.** Holsteinborg   **E.** Scoresbysund   **G.** Upernavik
B. Sukkertoppen   **D.** Angmagssalik   **F.** Julainehåb   **H.** Höfn

The capital of Greenland is _____; of Iceland is _____.

The _____ side of Greenland is more inhabited than the _____ side.
Locate the following Points of Interest. Write their numbers below next to the symbols that represent them on the map.

1. Radar Station at Thule   **4.** Icecap   **7.** Cape Brewster
2. Cape Morris Jesup   **5.** Mount Gunnbjorn   **8.** Cape York
3. North Pole   **6.** Cape Farewell   **9.** Disko Island

Mexico

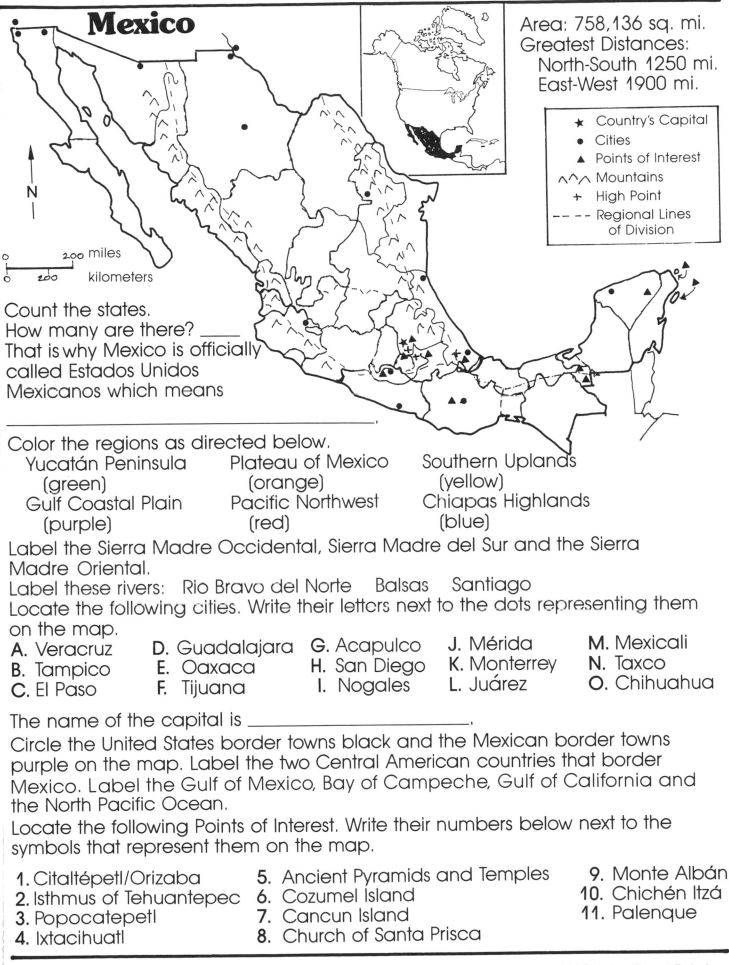

Area: 758,136 sq. mi.
Greatest Distances:
  North-South 1250 mi.
  East-West 1900 mi.

★ Country's Capital
● Cities
▲ Points of Interest
∧∧∧ Mountains
+ High Point
--- Regional Lines
    of Division

N

0   200 miles
0   200 kilometers

Count the states.
How many are there? ____
That is why Mexico is officially
called Estados Unidos
Mexicanos which means

_____

Color the regions as directed below.
  Yucatán Peninsula   Plateau of Mexico   Southern Uplands
    (green)   (orange)   (yellow)
  Gulf Coastal Plain   Pacific Northwest   Chiapas Highlands
    (purple)   (red)   (blue)

Label the Sierra Madre Occidental, Sierra Madre del Sur and the Sierra
Madre Oriental.
Label these rivers: Rio Bravo del Norte   Balsas   Santiago
Locate the following cities. Write their letters next to the dots representing them
on the map.

A. Veracruz   **D.** Guadalajara   **G.** Acapulco   **J.** Mérida   **M.** Mexicali
B. Tampico   **E.** Oaxaca   **H.** San Diego   **K.** Monterrey   **N.** Taxco
C. El Paso   **F.** Tijuana   **I.** Nogales   **L.** Juárez   **O.** Chihuahua

The name of the capital is _____.
Circle the United States border towns black and the Mexican border towns
purple on the map. Label the two Central American countries that border
Mexico. Label the Gulf of Mexico, Bay of Campeche, Gulf of California and
the North Pacific Ocean.
Locate the following Points of Interest. Write their numbers below next to the
symbols that represent them on the map.

1. Citaltépetl/Orizaba   **5.** Ancient Pyramids and Temples   **9.** Monte Albán
2. Isthmus of Tehuantepec   **6.** Cozumel Island   **10.** Chichén Itzá
3. Popocatepetl   **7.** Cancun Island   **11.** Palenque
4. Ixtacihuatl   **8.** Church of Santa Prisca

Central America

Area: 201,976 sq. mi.

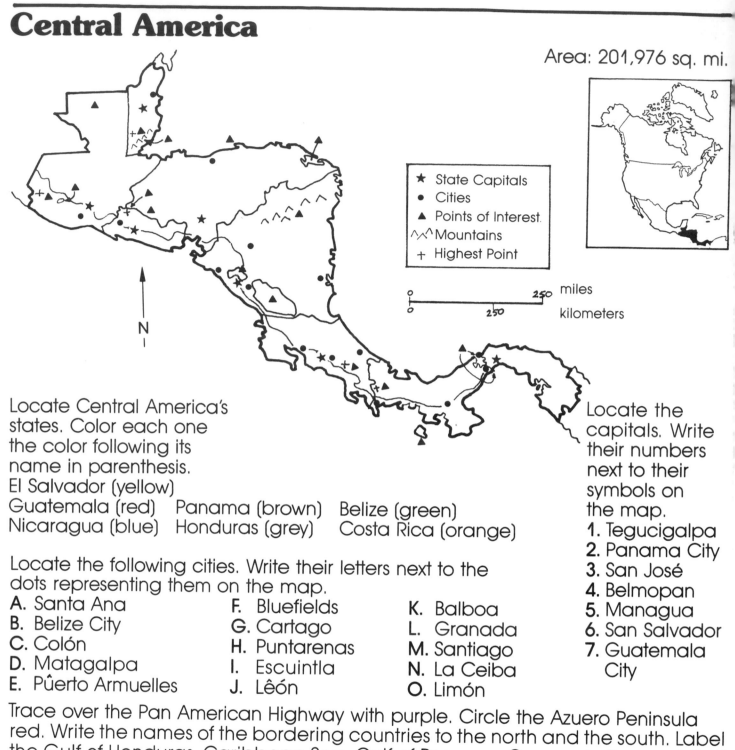

★ State Capitals
● Cities
▲ Points of Interest
∧∧^ Mountains
+ Highest Point

miles
kilometers

Locate Central America's states. Color each one the color following its name in parenthesis.
El Salvador (yellow)
Guatemala (red)   Panama (brown)   Belize (green)
Nicaragua (blue)   Honduras (grey)   Costa Rica (orange)

Locate the capitals. Write their numbers next to their symbols on the map.
1. Tegucigalpa
2. Panama City
3. San José
4. Belmopan
5. Managua
6. San Salvador
7. Guatemala City

Locate the following cities. Write their letters next to the dots representing them on the map.
A. Santa Ana
B. Belize City
C. Colón
D. Matagalpa
E. Pûerto Armuelles
F. Bluefields
G. Cartago
H. Puntarenas
I. Escuintla
J. Lêón
K. Balboa
L. Granada
M. Santiago
N. La Ceiba
O. Limón

Trace over the Pan American Highway with purple. Circle the Azuero Peninsula red. Write the names of the bordering countries to the north and the south. Label the Gulf of Honduras, Caribbean Sea, Gulf of Panama, Coronado Bay and Gulf of Fonseca.

Locate the following Points of Interest. Write their numbers next to the symbols that represent them.
8. Panama Canal
9. Volcán Barú
10. Coiba Island
11. Victoria Peak
12. Maya Mountains
13. Chirripó Grande
14. Cerros de Celaque Mountains
15. Laguna de Caratasca
16. Cabo de Honduras
17. Volcán Tajumulco
18. Tikal Ruins
19. Lago de Atitlán
20. Monte Cristo
21. Lago de Nicaragua
22. Lago de Managua
23. Cordillera Isabella Mountains

The Panama Canal

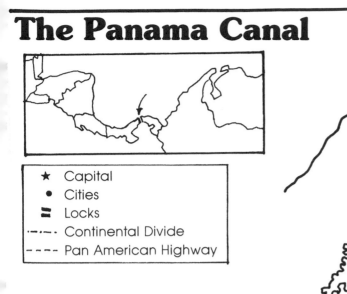

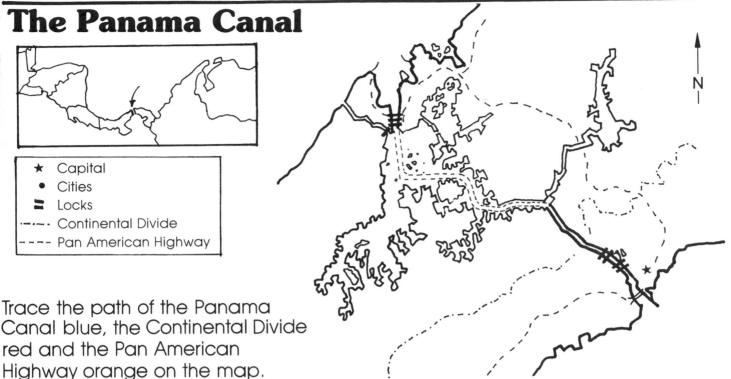

Legend:
- ★ Capital
- • Cities
- ≋ Locks
- ─·─·─ Continental Divide
- ─ ─ ─ Pan American Highway

Trace the path of the Panama Canal blue, the Continental Divide red and the Pan American Highway orange on the map.

Use the map and the geographic terms and locations in the box below to complete the paragraph under the box. It describes the landmarks a ship would pass in going from the Atlantic to the Pacific Ocean through the Panama Canal.

GEOGRAPHIC TERMS AND LOCATIONS

Gatun Lake   Gamboa   Thatcher Ferry Bridge   Pedro Miguel Locks   Colón
southeast   Cristóbal   Gatun Locks   Gaillard Cut   Gatun Dam   Gold Hill   northwest
Limón Bay   Bay of Panama   Contractor's Hill   Miraflores Lake   Miraflores Locks

---

A ship on the Atlantic Ocean enters the Panama Canal at the city of _____ by way of _____ which is the harbor for the town of _____. The ship travels through the bay to the _____. There, three locks raise the ship to the level of _____. The ship then sails past the _____ that holds back the Chagres River, across the lake to _____. Here the ship enters the eight mile, man-made _____ that goes between _____ on the east and _____ on the west. When the ship is at the end of the cut it enters the _____ which lower it to _____. The ship then travels across to the _____ which lower it to the level of the Pacific Ocean. Before it reaches the Pacific, the ship passes under the _____ and into the _____.
A ship going from the Atlantic Ocean to the Pacific travels from a _____ direction into a _____ one.

West Indies

Area: Approximately 2000 mi. long

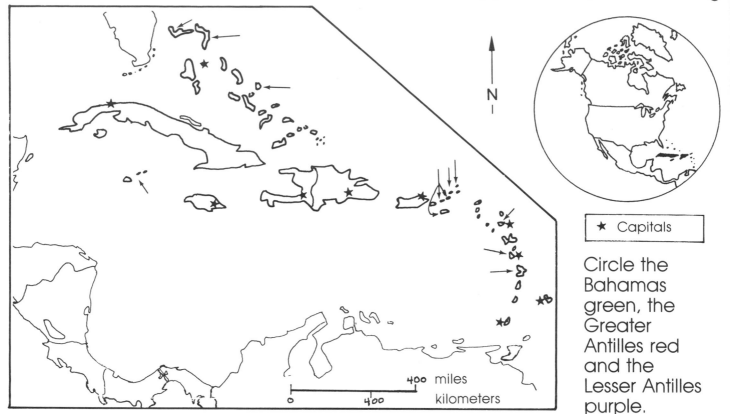

★ Capitals

Circle the Bahamas green, the Greater Antilles red and the Lesser Antilles purple.

Locate the following islands. Write their letters below in the correct places on the map.

A. Cuba
B. Andros
C. Grand Bahama
D. Great Abaco
E. San Salvador

F. Jamaica
G. Hispaniola
H. Puerto Rico
I. Virgin Islands
J. Dominica

K. Grenada
L. Barbados
M. Cayman Islands
N. Martinique
O. Antigua and Barbuda

Hispaniola is divided into two political countries. Label each one. Label the following bodies of water.

North Atlantic Ocean
Caribbean Sea

Straits of Florida
Gulf of Mexico

Mona Passage
Windward Passage

Circle the closest part of North America's mainland to the West Indies orange.

Circle the capital of the Bahamas yellow and write its name.

Locate the following capitals. Write their numbers next to the symbols representing them on the map.

1. Santo Domingo
2. San Juan
3. Havana

4. Port-au-Prince
5. Kingston
6. St. Johns

7. Bridgetown
8. St. George's
9. Roseau

Label the following bordering countries of the West Indies region:
United States   Honduras   Nicaragua   Venezuela   Costa Rica   Colombia

With a brown pencil, draw the route you would travel on a cruise ship from Miami to Caracus.

Facts About North America

Draw a line from the number on the left to the fact it tells about on the right.

7,071,000	Distance in miles of Panama Canal
12,000	Year Panama Canal was built
49	Number of states in U.S. on the North American continent
10	Highest waterfall in North America, Yosemite Falls
7	Approximate number of ships that pass through the Panama Canal in a year
440	North America's largest city, New York
50.72	Number of states in Central America
1999	Years it took to build the Panama Canal
11	Percent of land covered by ice in Greenland
20,320	Year Panama will take over the management of the Panama Canal
1914	Feet below sea level of North America's lowest point, Death Valley
1,071	Number of countries in North America
80	Highest point in North America, Mt. McKinley
31,700	Square miles of North America's largest lake, Superior
282	Miles northernmost Greenland is from North Pole
2,425	Miles of North America's longest river, Mackenzie

Classify the places named in the box below. Write their names after the type of feature that is listed below the box.

Chihuahuan	Rio Grande	Cuba	Cascade	Mojave	White
Greenland	Arkansas	Aleutians	Michigan		Sonoran
Okeechobee	Bermuda	Sierra Madre	Mackenzie		St. Lawrence

ISLANDS_____

LAKES_____

RIVERS_____

MOUNTAIN RANGES_____

DESERTS_____

If you were a bird and could fly a direct route from each of the following, over what countries would you fly?

1. Mexico City to Quebec_____

2. Salt Lake City to Virginia Beach_____

3. Toronto to Anchorage_____

4. New York to Cristóbal Colón _____

5. St. Paul to Guatemala City_____

Northern South America

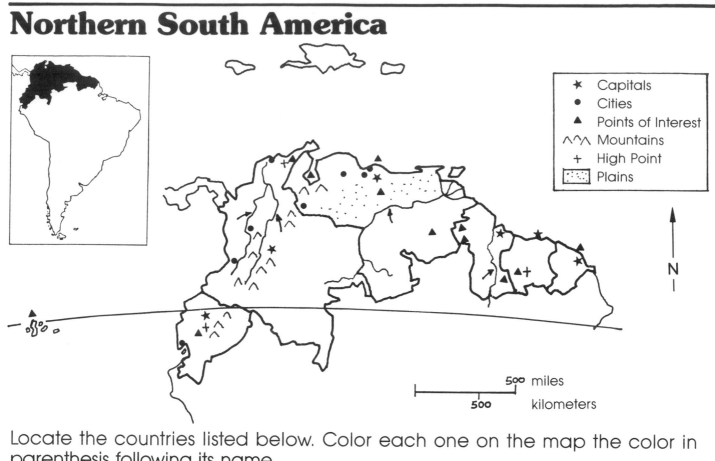

Locate the countries listed below. Color each one on the map the color in parenthesis following its name.

French Guiana (red)   Suriname (yellow)   Guyana (blue)
Venezuela (green)   Colombia (purple)   Ecuador (orange)

Write the name of each country's capital next to the symbol representing it on the map.

Bogotá   Quito   Cayenne   Georgetown   Paramaribo   Caracas

Label the Magdalena (**A**), Cauca (**B**), Orinoco (**C**) and Essequibo (**D**) Rivers.

Locate the following cities. Write their letters next to the dots representing them on the map.

E. Santa Marta   **G.** San Cristóbal   **I.** Guayaquil   **K.** Cali
F. Barquisimeto   **H.** Valencia   **J.** Medellin   **L.** Maracay

Locate the following Points of Interest. Write the numbers next to the symbols representing them on the map.

1. Devils Island   **5.** King Edward VII Falls   **9.** Mt. Juliana Top
2. Cape Codero   **6.** King George VI Falls   **10.** Lake Maracaibo
3. The Llanos   **7.** Great Falls   **11.** Angel Falls
4. Galapagos Islands   **8.** Chimborazo Volcano   **12.** Cristóbal Colón

Through what countries does the Equator run in this part of South America?

_____

Label the following bodies of water:

North Pacific Ocean   Atlantic Ocean   Gulf of Venezuela
Caribbean Sea   Gulf of Panama   Gulf of Darién

Central South America

Legend:
- ★ Capitals
- • Cities
- ▲ Points of Interest
- + High Point
- ∧∧∧ Mountains
- Amazon Region
- Northeast Region
- Central and Southern Plateaus

Locate the countries listed below.
Color each one on the map the
color in parenthesis following
its name.

Brazil (orange)   Peru (brown)   Bolivia (green)

Name the three geographic regions of Brazil. _____

Through what country does the Equator extend?_____

Write the name of each country's capital next to the symbol representing it on
the map.
Which country has two capitals? _____ Why? _____

Trace the Amazon River with blue. Some of the rivers that feed the Amazon are
lettered in circles on the map. Write the name of the river next to its letter below.

N _____   Q _____   T _____

O _____   R _____   U _____

P _____   S _____   V _____

Locate the following cities. Write the letters representing them next to the dots .
A. Cusco   **B.** Rio de Janeiro **C.** Manaus   **D.** São Paulo   **E.** Nauta   **F.** Iquitos
G. São Luis **H.** Salvador   **I.** Arequipa **J.** Pôrto Alegre **K.** Huancayo **L.** San José

Locate the following Points of Interest. Write their numbers next to the symbols that
represent them on the map.
1. Salar de Uyuni
2. Bañadas del Izozog
3. Chanchan
4. Pachacamac
5. Nazca Lines
6. Machu Picchu
7. Sacsahuaman
8. Lake Poopó
9. Guiana Highlands
10. Brazilian Highlands
11. Iguacu Falls
12. Selvas
13. Lake Titicaca
14. Pico da Neblina
15. Huascarán

500 miles
500 kilometers

N

Southern South America

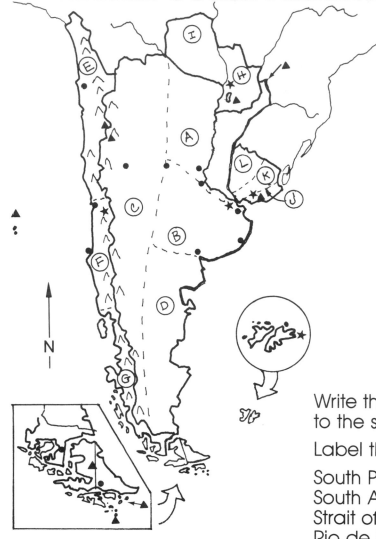

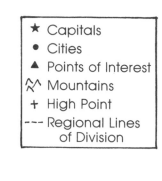

★ Capitals
● Cities
▲ Points of Interest
⋏⋏ Mountains
+ High Point
--- Regional Lines of Division

0 ————— 500 miles
0 ————— 500 kilometers

Locate the countries listed below. Color each one on the map the color in parenthesis following its name.

Argentina (red)   Falkland Islands
Uruguay (green)   (brown)
Paraguay (orange)   Chile (yellow)

Write the name of each country's capital next to the symbol representing it on the map.

Label the following bodies of water.

South Pacific Ocean   Paraguay River
South Atlantic Ocean   Uruguay River
Strait of Magellan   Paraná River
Rio de la Plata   Pilcomayo River

Each mainland country in this part of South America is divided into geographic regions. They are lettered in circles on the map. Write the name of each region for each country next to its letter below.

Argentina A. _____ B. _____ C. _____
D. _____ Chile E. _____ F. _____
G. _____ Paraguay H. _____ I. _____
Uruguay J. _____ K. _____ L. _____

Locate the following cities. Write their numbers next to the dots representing them on the map.

1. Antofagasta   4. Santa Fe   7. Valparaíso   10. Córdoba
2. La Plata   5. San Juan   8. Ushuaia   11. Punta Arenas
3. Rosario   6. Talcahuano   9. Bahía Blanca   12. Mar del Plata

Locate the following Points of Interest. Write their letters next to the symbols that represent them on the map.

A. Ojos del Salado   D. Juan Fernández Islands   G. Iguacu Falls
B. Tierra del Fuego   E. Aconcagua   H. Mirador Nacíonal
C. Cape Horn   F. Beagle Channel Islands   I. Lake Verá

Facts About South America

List the countries of South America in order of their physical size. Write the name of each country's capital after it.

Country   Capital   Country   Capital

1. _____
2. _____
3. _____
4. _____
5. _____
6. _____
7. _____

8. _____
9. _____
10. _____
11. _____
12. _____
13. _____
14. _____

Which two countries are under political rule other than that of South American governments? _____

What is the highest point in South America and where is it located?

_____

What is the lowest point in South America and where is it located?

_____

What is the southernmost city in South America? _____

What island 2,000 miles from shore is a part of Chile? _____

Which South American countries have no ocean coastline? _____

Which countries' coastlines touch more than one major ocean? _____

What is South America's largest lake and where is it located? _____

What is South America's highest large lake and where is it located?

_____

What is South America's longest river? _____ How does it rank in size when compared with other rivers in the world? _____ Where does it originate? _____

Where does it end? _____

Approximately how many islands are in the Falkland Islands group? _____

If you were a bird and could fly a direct route, over what countries would you fly?

1. Lake Maracaibo to Lake Titicaca _____
2. The Falklands to the Galapagos Islands _____
3. Callao to Salvador _____
4. Georgetown to Tierra del Fuego _____
5. Porto Alegre to Belém _____
6. Barranquilla to La Plata _____
7. Santiago to Fortaleza _____

The British Isles

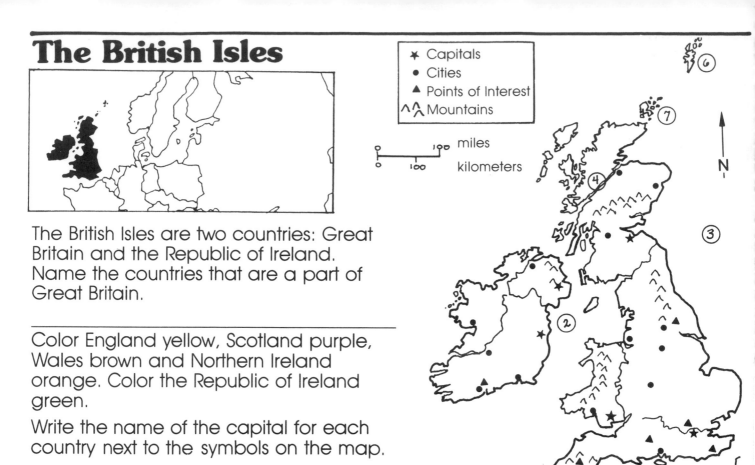

Capitals ★
Cities ●
Points of Interest ▲
Mountains ∧∧

100 miles
100 kilometers

The British Isles are two countries: Great Britain and the Republic of Ireland. Name the countries that are a part of Great Britain.

_____

Color England yellow, Scotland purple, Wales brown and Northern Ireland orange. Color the Republic of Ireland green.

Write the name of the capital for each country next to the symbols on the map.

Tell what each place listed below is and to what country it belongs.

Place	Geographic Feature	Country	Place	Geographic Feature	Country
Guernsey	_____	_____	Cambrians	_____	_____
Shannon	_____	_____	Hebrides	_____	_____
Grampians	_____	_____	Loch Ness	_____	_____
Thames	_____	_____			

Locate the following cities. Write their letters next to the symbols representing them on the map. Which one is a capital? _____

A. Cork
B. Leeds
C. London
D. Waterford
E. Glasgow
F. Liverpool
G. Swansea
H. Limerick
I. Aberdeen
J. Londonderry
K. Galway
L. Inverness
M. Southampton
N. Birmingham
O. Sheffield

The following bodies of water and island groups are numbered and circled on the map. Write the name of each next to its number below.

1._____   3._____   6._____
2._____   4._____   7._____
                          5._____

Locate the following Points of Interest. Write their numbers below next to the symbols that represent them on the map.

1. York Minster Cathedral
2. Blarney Stone
3. White Cliffs of Dover
4. Buckingham Palace
5. Stonehenge
6. Plymouth

Northern Europe

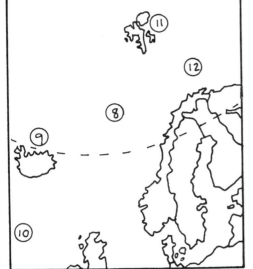

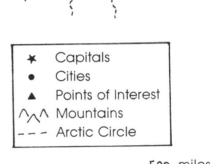

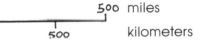

Trace over the Arctic Circle with black.
Color the Northern European countries on the
map the color in parenthesis following their
names:
Sweden (brown), Denmark (purple), Iceland
(red), Finland (green) and Norway (orange).

Locate the following cities. Write their letters next
to the symbols representing them on the map.

A. Trondheim	E. Turku	H. Helsinki
B. Reykjavik	F. Malmö	I. Stavanger
C. Copenhagen	G. Bergen	J. Stockholm
D. Oslo		K. Göteborg

Symbol	Legend
★	Capitals
●	Cities
▲	Points of Interest
∧∧∧	Mountains
- - -	Arctic Circle

0 ———————————————— 500 miles

0 ———————————————— 500 kilometers

Write the name of the capital for each country under its name below.

Norway   **Sweden**   **Finland**   **Iceland**   **Denmark**

The following bodies of water and islands are numbered and circled on the
map. Write the name of each next to its number below.

1 _____   5 _____   9 _____

2 _____   6 _____   10 _____

3 _____   7 _____   11 _____

4 _____   8 _____   12 _____

Locate the following Points of Interest. Write their numbers below next to the
symbols that represent them on the map.

1. Mt. Hekla	4. Gullfoss	7. Mt. Kebnekaise	10. Lake District
2. Geysir	5. Jostedal Glacier	8. Lake Vänern	
3. Dettifoss	6. Sogne Fiord	9. Lake Vättern	

France and a Neighbor

The following bodies of water are numbered and circled on the map. Write the name of each next to its number below.

1. _____
2. _____   9. _____
3. _____   10. _____
4. _____   11. _____
5. _____   12. _____
6. _____   13. _____
7. _____   14. _____
8. _____   15. _____

★ Capitals   ▲ Points of Interest
● Cities   ∧∧∧ Mountains

The capital of France is _____ and of Monaco is _____. To whom does Corsica belong? _____

Locate the following cities. Write their letters next to the dots representing them on the map.

A. Marseille   **D.** Bordeaux   **G.** Nice   **J.** Monaco   **M.** Strasbourg
B. Lyon   **E.** Lourdes   **H.** Nancy   **K.** Limoges   **N.** Grenoble
C. Paris   **F.** Le Havre   **I.** Orléans   **L.** Dijon   **O.** Toulouse

Circle the Pyrenees Mountains purple, the Jura Mountains red and the French Alps green.

Locate the following Points of Interest. Write the numbers below next to the symbols that represent them on the map.

1. Amphitheater of Nîmes   **4.** Mont Blanc   **7.** Eiffel Tower
2. Abbey at Mont-St-Michel   **5.** Châteaux de Blois   **8.** Louvre
3. Cathedral at Chartres   **6.** Versailles

Are any of the French places' names familiar to you? ____ If yes, which ones and where do you think you may have seen their name before? _____

_____

The Netherlands, Belgium and Luxembourg

Legend:
- ✶ Capitals
- • Cities
- ▲ Points of Interest
- ∿ Canals

N

```
0        50  miles
├────┼────┤
0        50
         kilometers
```

Color Belgium grey, Luxembourg yellow and The Netherlands brown. Color the IJsselmeer blue. Trace over the rivers with blue. Number each one on the map the same as its number below.

1. Maas(Meuse) 4. Leie   7. Sambre
2. Rhine (Waal) 5. Rhine (Lek) 8. Vecht
3. Schelde   6. IJssel

What rivers form Luxembourg's eastern border?_____

Locate the following cities. Write their letters next to the dots representing them on the map.

A. Mons   H. Haarlem   O. Luxembourg
B. Liege   I. Antwerp   P. Enschede
C. Ghent   J. Brussels   Q. The Hague
D. Bruges   K. Genk   R. Utrecht
E. Ostend   L. Nijmegen   S. Eindhoven
F. Arnhem   M. Amsterdam
G. Tilburg   N. Groningen

Write the names of the capitals and their countries found on the map.

1. _____
2. _____
3. _____

Locate the following Points of Interest. Write their numbers below next to the symbols that represent them on the map.

9. Parliament
10. Anne Frank's House
11. Europoort (largest port)
12. Cathedral of Notre Dame
13. Afsluitdijk-Barrier Dam
14. Waddenzee
15. Hoek van Holland

East and West Germany

Legend:
- ★ Capitals
- ● Cities
- ▲ Points of Interest
- --- City Boundary
- ∧∧∧ Mountains
- + Highest Point
- +++ Berlin Wall

Color East Germany orange and West Germany red. Label the North Sea and Baltic Sea and color them blue on the map. Circle the Bavarian Alps blue and the Harz Mountains green. Color the city of Berlin, East and West, green. Trace over the Berlin Wall with black.

100 miles
100 kilometers

The following rivers are numbered and circled on the map. Write the name of each next to its number below.

1. _____   4. _____   7. _____
2. _____   5. _____   8. _____
3. _____   6. _____   9. _____

Locate the following cities. Write their letters next to the symbols representing them on the map.

A. Magdeburg   E. East Berlin   I. Bremen   M. Hannover   Q. Dortmund
B. Karl-Marx-Stadt F. Nuremburg   J. Worms   N. Leipzig   R. Heidelberg
C. Frankfurt   G. Munich   K. Bonn   O. Hamburg   S. Mainz
D. Düsseldorf   H. Dresden   L. Cologne   P. Stuttgart   T. Duisburg

The capital of East Germany is _____, of West Germany is _____

Locate the following Points of Interest. Write their numbers below next to the symbols that represent them on the map.

1. The Black Forest   3. Zugspitze   5. Potsdam
2. Lake Constance   4. Fichtel-berg   6. Ruhr Valley

On the back of this page tell why Berlin and Germany are divided.

The Iberian Peninsula

The Iberian Peninsula consists of three countries: Spain, Portugal, and Andorra and a British dependency, Gibraltar. Color Spain green, Portugal orange, Andorra purple and circle Gibraltar purple.

* Capitals
• Cities
∧∧ Mountains

Locate the following cities. Write their letters next to the symbols representing them.

A. Barcelona	C. Toledo	E. Palma	G. Andorra	I. Porto	K. Córdoba
B. Lisbon	D. Granada	F. Malaga	H. Valencia	J. Seville	L. Madrid

Write the capital of each country below under the country's name.

Spain	**Portugal**	**Andorra**	**Balearic Islands**

Name the three main islands that comprise the Balearic Islands.

_____ Circle them.

Trace over the Tagus (1), Guadalquiver (2), and Ebro (3) Rivers with blue. Then, number them. Number each mountain range on the map as follows: Sierra Nevada (4), Pyrenees (5), Cantábrica (6), Sierra Morena (7), Serra da Estrela (8).

Number each body of water: Mediterranean Sea (9), North Atlantic Ocean (10), Gulf of Cádiz (11), Bay of Biscay (12).

Name three island groups that belong to Portugal or Spain, but are not pictured on the map. Write their name, location and to which country they belong on the following chart.

Island Group	Location	Country

Italy and Its Neighbors

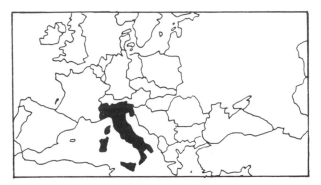

Color Italy green, Sicily orange and Sardinia grey.

Label the Ligurian Sea, Adriatic Sea, Mediterranean Sea and the Tyrrhanian Sea. Color the seas blue.

Circle the Italian Alps blue and the Apennines black.

Trace over the three most important rivers with blue. They are numbered and circled on the map. Write the name of each next to its number below.

1. _____ 2. _____ 3. _____

Locate the following cities. Write their letters next to the dots representing them on the map.

A. Rome   E. Florence   I. Valletta
B. Vatican City F. Bologna   J. Genoa
C. San Marino   G. Palermo   K. Milan
D. Naples   H. Trieste   L. Venice

Name the three capitals above and write the name of the country for which they are the capitals.

1. _____

2. _____

3. _____

Which city mentioned in the group of cities is a state?

_____

Legend

★ Capitals	▲ Points of Interest
• Cities	∧∧∧ Mountains

Which of Italy's neighbors are independent countries? _____

_____

To what country do Sicily and

Sardinia belong? _____

Corsica? _____

Locate the following Points of Interest. Write their numbers below next to the symbols that represent them on the map.

1. Mt. Blanc   6. Terni Waterfall
2. Vesuvius   7. Colosseum
3. Mt. Etna   8. St. Peters
4. Capri   9. Leaning Tower
5. Lake Como   of Pisa

Switzerland, Austria and Liechtenstein

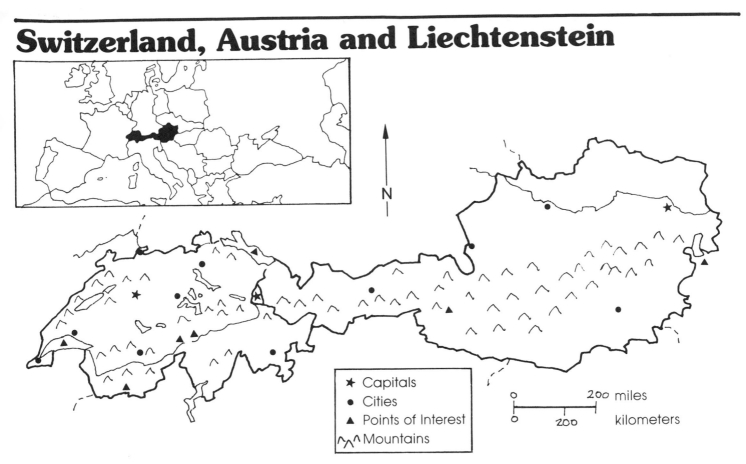

* ★ Capitals
* • Cities
* ▲ Points of Interest
* ᴧᴧᴧ Mountains

0 —————— 200 miles
0 —————— 200 kilometers

Color Switzerland green, Austria red and Liechtenstein yellow. Trace over the Danube River blue.

Circle the Swiss Alps brown, the Austrian Alps black and the Jura Mountains red.

What forms Liechtenstein's western border? _____

Locate the following cities. Write their letters next to the symbols representing them on the map.

A. Salzburg	**E.** Bern	**H.** Lucerne	**K.** Interlaken
B. Innsbruck	**F.** Linz	**I.** Zürich	**L.** Geneva
C. Lausanne	**G.** Graz	**J.** Vienna	**M.** Basel
D. St. Moritz			**N.** Vaduz

Name the three capitals above and write the name of the country for which each is the capital after its name.

1. _____ 2. _____ 3. _____

Locate the following Points of Interest. Write their numbers below next to the symbols that represent them on the map.

1. Start of the Rhône	**3.** Grossglockner	**6.** Lake Constance
2. Start of the Rhine	**4.** Mattêrhorn	**7.** Lake Geneva
	5. Neusiedler Lake	

Write the name of all the bordering countries to these three countries on the map.

The Balkan Peninsula

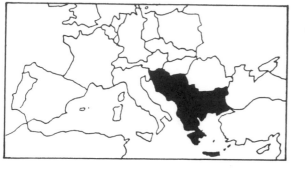

Legend:
* ★ Capitals
* ● Cities
* ▲ Points of Interest
* ⋀⋀⋀ Mountain Ranges

Color the Balkan countries on the map the color in parenthesis following their names in the sentence below.

The Balkan Peninsula includes Greece (orange), most of Yugoslavia (red), the eastern part of Turkey (green), Bulgaria* (grey) and Albania* (brown).

N

100 miles

100 kilometers

Write the name of the capital for each country under its name below.
Write the capital's letter below next to the symbol representing it on the map.

Yugoslavia	Greece	Bulgaria	Albania	Turkey
A. _____	B. _____	C. _____	D. _____	E. _____

Locate the following cities. Write their letters next to the dots representing them on the map.

- **F.** Istanbul
- **G.** Delphi
- **H.** Zagreb
- **I.** Thessaloniki
- **J.** Olympia
- **K.** Sarajevo
- **L.** Skopje
- **M.** Sparti

The following bodies of water are numbered and circled on the map. Write the name of each body of water next to its number below.

1 _____   3 _____   5 _____   7 _____

2 _____   4 _____   6 _____   8 _____

Circle the Aegean Islands yellow and the Ionian Islands green. Locate the following Points of Interest. Write their numbers below next to the symbols that represent them on the map.

- **1.** The Dardanelles
- **2.** The Acropolis
- **3.** Mt. Musala
- **4.** Corfu
- **5.** Mt. Olympus
- **6.** Dinaric Alps
- **7.** Crete
- **8.** Balkan Mts.
- **9.** Bosporus
- **10.** Pindus Mts.
- **11.** Piraeus
- **12.** Gulf of Corinth

*Bulgaria and Albania are also included in Eastern Europe.

Eastern Europe

★	Capitals
●	Cities
▲	Points of Interest
∧∧∧	Mountains
+	Highest Point

The east European countries are numbered on the map. Write the name of each country after its number below. Color the country the color in parentheses after its number. Name the capital of each country.

	Country	Capital
1. (orange)		
2. (red)		
3. (green)		
4. (yellow)		
5. (brown)		
6. (purple)		

Which east European countries are surrounded by other countries? _____

_____ Tell what large bodies of water touch a border of the

other east European countries and which countries they touch. _____

_____

_____

Trace over the Danube with blue. It forms partial borders for what countries?

_____

Where does it terminate? _____
By which countries is Albania separated from the other east European countries?

_____

Locate the following Points of Interest. Write their numbers below next to the symbols that represent them on the map.

1. Mount Kékes
2. Tatras Mountains
3. Mount Moldoveanu
4. Gellert Baths
5. Mineral Baths at Mariánské Lázně

6. Lake Balaton
7. Mouths of the Danube
8. Botev Peak
9. City: Gdańsk
10. Mount Korabit

11. Resort at Varna
12. Rysy Peak
13. Gerlachovka
14. City: Kraków
15. Mineral baths at Karlovy Vary

Southwest Asia

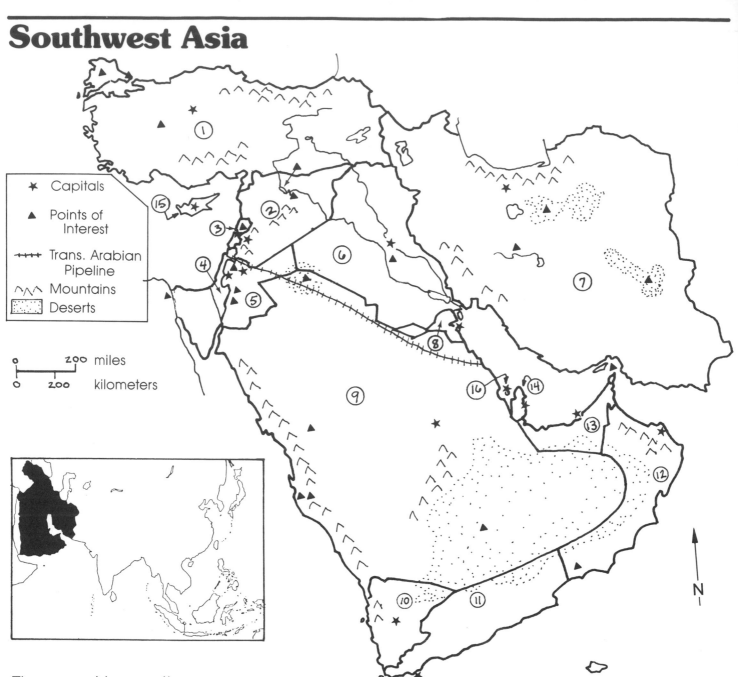

The countries on the map are numbered and circled. Write their names next to their numbers below. After each country's name, write the name of its capital.

1. _____   9. _____
2. _____   10. _____
3. _____   11. _____
4. _____   12. _____
5. _____   13. _____
6. _____   14. _____
7. _____   15. _____
8. _____   16. _____

Southwest Asia (continued)

Which are island countries?_____

Which are peninsulas?_____

Color the country of Oman red. What is unusual about its boundaries?_____

_____

Trace over the Tigris and Euphrates Rivers with blue. Where do they start?_____

_____

Where do they end?_____

Name some ports on the Iranian side of the Persian Gulf._____

_____

 On the Arabian side?_____

_____

What are the names of the three islands belonging to Yemen P.D.R.?

_____ Circle them orange.

Label the following mountain ranges on the map.
    Hejaz   Al Hajar   Anti Lebanon   Asir
    Zagros   Tuwayq   Elburz

Trace over the Trans-Arabrian Pipeline with green. What good is this pipeline?

_____

Locate the following Points of Interest. Write their numbers below next to the
symbols that represent them on the map.

1. Ancient Babylon
2. Rub Al Khali Desert
3. Frankincense trees in the
   Dhofar Region
4. Persepolis (Ancient Persia)
5. Holy City: Mecca
6. Dasht-E Kavir (Great Salt Desert)
7. Crusader Castle at Al Karak
8. Suez Canal
9. Temple at Baalbek
10. Assad Reservoir
11. Strait of Hormuz
12. Ancient Istanbul - Constantinople
13. Royal Palace in Jidda
14. Holy City: Modina
15. Dasht-E Lut (Great Sand Desert)
16. Jericho
17. Petra
18. Syrian Desert
19. Thrace (Europe portion)
20. Anatolia (Asian portion)
21. Tabka Dam

South Asia

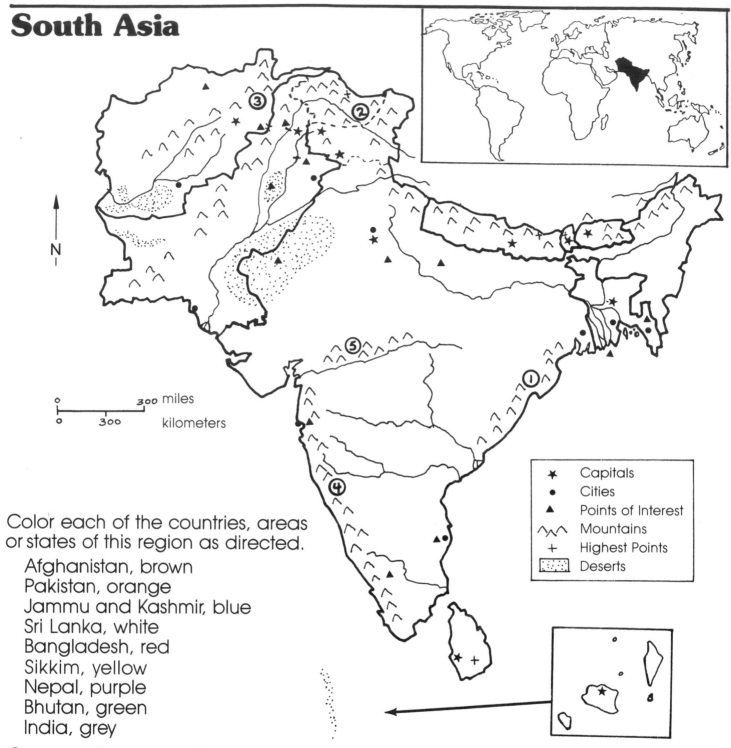

Color each of the countries, areas or states of this region as directed.

Afghanistan, brown
Pakistan, orange
Jammu and Kashmir, blue
Sri Lanka, white
Bangladesh, red
Sikkim, yellow
Nepal, purple
Bhutan, green
India, grey

Legend:
- ★ Capitals
- • Cities
- ▲ Points of Interest
- ⌃⌃⌃ Mountains
- + Highest Points
- ⬚ Deserts

Cross out the name of the state in the above list. Draw a line under the name of the area in dispute between Pakistan and India.

Locate the following cities. Write their letters next to the symbols representing them on the map.

A. Bombay
B. Srinagar
C. Male
D. Kabul
E. Colombo
F. Barisal

G. Karachi
H. New Delhi
I. Islamabad
J. Chittagong
K. Dhaka

L. Madras
M. Kathmandu
N. Calcutta
O. Qandahar
P. Delhi

Q. Gangtok
R. Lahore
S. Thimphu
T. Jammu

South Asia (continued)

Fill in the chart below. List the countries in order of their physical size. List Sikkum and Jammu and Kashmir last.

Country	Capital	Country	Capital

Trace over the following rivers with blue. After their names below write what countries they cross in this region.

Ganges _____   Indus _____

Brahmaputra _____   Helmand _____

Krishna, Godavari and Cauvery _____

Locate the following Points of Interest. Write their numbers next to the symbols that represent them on the map.

1. Elephanta Caves
2. Mouths of the Ganges
3. Karnaphuli Reservoir
4. Thal Desert
5. Thar Desert

6. Mangla Dam
7. Tarbela Dam
8. Khyber Pass
9. Nilgiri Hills

10. Taj Mahal
11. University of Lucknow
12. Hindu Temple in Madras
13. Blue Mosque in
      Mazar-e Sharif

In what countries and areas of this region are the Himalayas?

_____

List the three highest mountains in this region, and in the world, in order. Tell where they are located.

1. _____

2. _____

3. _____

There are other mountain ranges in this region. They are numbered and circled on the map. Write their names next to their numbers below.

1. _____   3. _____

2. _____   4. _____

5. _____

Israel

Area: 8,019 sq. mi. Greatest Distances: North-South 256 mi. East-West 81 mi.

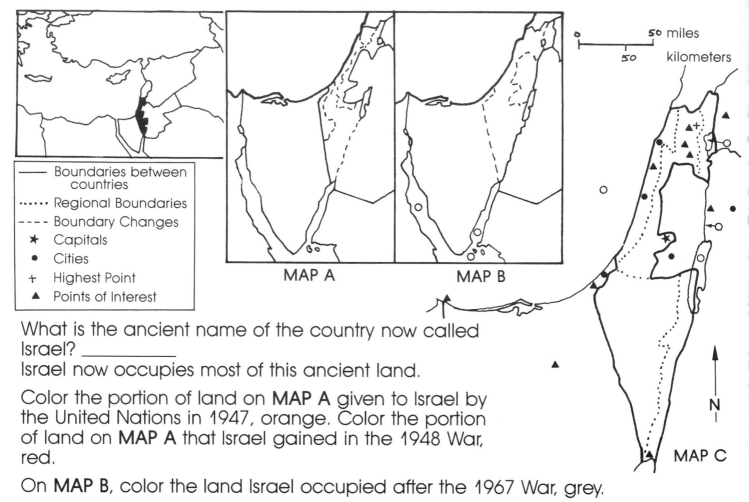

Legend:
— Boundaries between countries
····· Regional Boundaries
- - - Boundary Changes
★ Capitals
• Cities
+ Highest Point
▲ Points of Interest

MAP A   MAP B   MAP C

What is the ancient name of the country now called Israel? _____
Israel now occupies most of this ancient land.

Color the portion of land on **MAP A** given to Israel by the United Nations in 1947, orange. Color the portion of land on **MAP A** that Israel gained in the 1948 War, red.

On **MAP B**, color the land Israel occupied after the 1967 War, grey.

Since 1975, Israel has withdrawn from much of the territory until it looks like it does in **MAP C**. Write in the names of Israel's bordering countries on **MAP C**. Color Israel's land regions the color after each region's name in parenthesis on **MAP C**.

Coastal Plains (red)	Negev Desert (yellow)
Rift Valley (green)	Judeo-Galilean Highlands (orange)

Locate the following cities. Write their letters next to the symbols representing them on the map.

A. Jerusalem   **B.** Haifa   **C.** Gaza   **D.** Tel Aviv-Yafo   **E.** Bethlehem   **F.** Amman

The capital of Israel is _____.
Locate the following bodies of water. Color them blue and write their letters next to the dots [o] representing them on **MAP B** and **MAP C**.

G. Jordon River   **H.** Sea of Galilee   **I.** Gulf of Aqaba   **J.** Mediterranean
K. Dead Sea   **L.** Gulf of Suez   **M.** Red Sea   Sea

Locate the following Points of Interest. Write their numbers below next to the symbols that represent them on **MAP C**.

1. Elat	**4.** Sinai Peninsula	**7.** Golan Heights	**10.** Suez Canal
2. Nazareth	**5.** Galilee	**8.** Lowest land in world	
3. Mount Meron	**6.** Gaza Strip	**9.** Plain of Sharon	

China, Mongolia and Taiwan

* Capitals
* Cities
▲ Points of Interest
∧∧∧ Mountains
+ Highest Point
⊖ Lowest Point
▢ Deserts
▢ Other Political Units
ⴖⴖⴖ Great Wall

250   500 miles

250 500   kilometers

Color Mongolia yellow,
China green and Taiwan red.
Label the two political units on the map that are not under the Chinese government's jurisdiction, but are on its mainland.
Locate the following cities. Write their letters next to the symbols representing them on the map.

A. Tientsin	D. Beijing	G. Ch'ung-Ch'ing	J. Ulan Bator
B. Taipei	E. Harbin	H. Shen-yang	K. Wu-han
C. Canton	F. Hang-chou	I. Shanghai	L. Nan-ching

Write the name below of each country's capital after the country's name.

Mongolia_____ China_____ Taiwan_____

The following mountain ranges are numbered and circled on the map.
Write the name of each next to its number below.

1. _____   3. _____   5. _____   7. _____   9. _____

2. _____   4. _____   6. _____   8. _____   10. _____

Label the deserts on the map.

Make an X where each of the following rivers begin.

Brahmaputra   Mekong   Salween   Yangtze   Huang Ho   Indus

Trace over each one's path with blue as it travels across China. Where did they all begin? _____

Locate the following Points of Interest. Write their numbers below next to the symbols representing them on the map.

1. The Great Wall of China	3. Turfan Depression	5. Potala Palace
2. Mount Everest	4. Feng-hsien Cave	6. Hai-nan

Union of Soviet Socialist Republics

The U.S.S.R. is the world's largest country. It spreads over a part of Europe and Asia from the _____ Sea to the _____ Ocean.

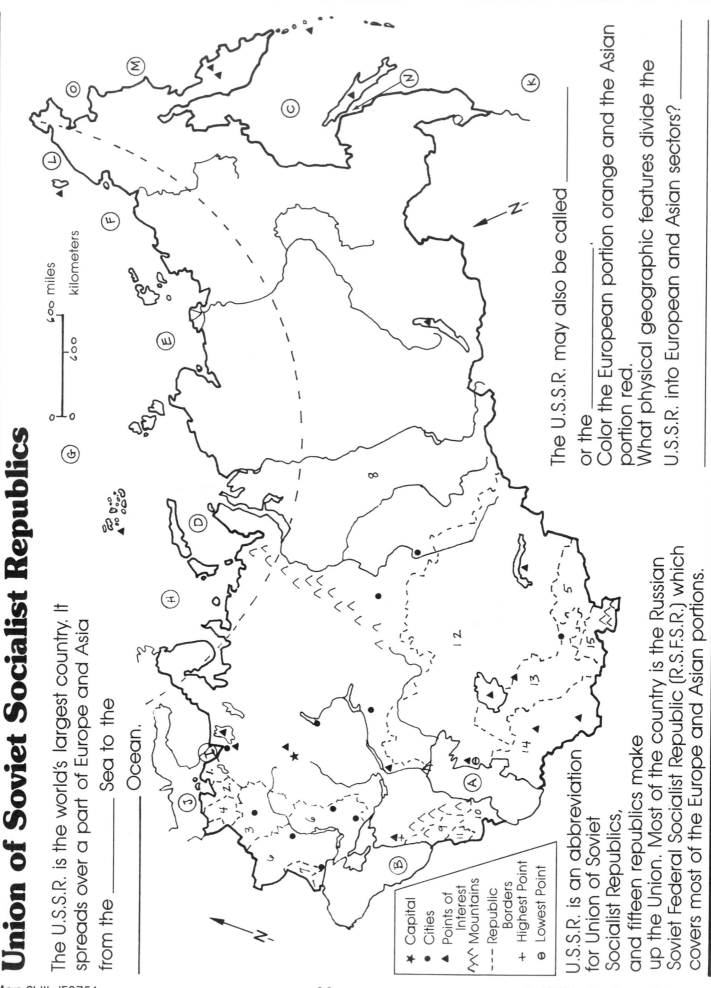

The U.S.S.R. may also be called _____ or the _____.
Color the European portion orange and the Asian portion red.
What physical geographic features divide the U.S.S.R. into European and Asian sectors? _____

U.S.S.R. is an abbreviation for Union of Soviet Socialist Republics, and fifteen republics make up the Union. Most of the country is the Russian Soviet Federal Socialist Republic (R.S.F.S.R.) which covers most of the Europe and Asian portions.

Legend:
★ Capital
● Cities
◤ Points of Interest
⋏⋏ Mountains
--- Republic Borders
+ Highest Point
⊖ Lowest Point

The U.S.S.R. (continued)

The fifteen republics are numbered on the map. Write their number next to their name below.

___ Georgian   ___ Kirghiz
___ Lithuanian   ___ Armenian
___ Estonian   ___ Byelorussian
___ Tajik   ___ R.S.F.S.R.
___ Azerbaijan   ___ Latvian
___ Kazakh   ___ Uzbek
___ Turkmen   ___ Moldavian
___ Ukrainian

Trace over the following rivers and label them on the map.

Ob   Don   Yenisey   Volga   Lena   Dnepr

Circle the Caucasus Mountains purple, the Ural Mountains red and the Pamirs green.

Locate the following cities. Write their letters next to the symbols representing them on the map.

A. Gorki   D. Moscow   G. Sverdlovsk   J. Odessa
B. Minsk   E. Kharkov   H. Tashkent   K. Omsk
C. Kiev   F. Leningrad   I. Kuybyshev   L. Donetsk

The capital of Russia is _____.

Locate the following Points of Interest. Write their numbers below next to the symbols that represent them on the map.

1. Kara Kum Desert   10. Klyuchevskaya Volcano
2. Eternal Flame Monument   11. Lake Balkhash
3. The Hermitage   12. The Karagiye Depression
4. The Kremlin   13. Wrangel Island
5. Mount Elbrus   14. The Merv
6. Aral Sea   15. Franz Josef Land
7. Kyzyl Kum Desert   16. Lake Ladoga
8. Lake Baikal   17. Kuril Islands
9. Kamchatka Peninsula   18. Sakhalin

The following bodies of water are lettered on the map. Write their letters next to their names below.

___ Arctic Ocean   ___ Laptev Sea   ___ Sea of Okhotsk
___ Caspian Sea   ___ Gulf of Finland   ___ Tatar Strait
___ Barents Sea   ___ Baltic Sea   ___ Sea of Japan
___ Gulf of Anadyr   ___ Black Sea   ___ Kara Sea
___ East Siberian Sea   ___ Chukchi Sea   ___ Bering Sea

Southeast Asia

Color each country of Southeast Asia
the color following its name.
Philippines, blue   Kampuchea, brown
Malaysia, grey   Singapore, purple
Indonesia, tan   Thailand, green
Brunei, white   Burma, red
Vietnam, orange   Laos, yellow
Another name for Kampuchea is
_____

After each country's name, write the
name of its capital.

Burma _____
Laos _____
Thailand _____
Philippines _____
Singapore _____
Brunei _____
Kampuchea _____
Vietnam _____
Malaysia _____
Indonesia _____

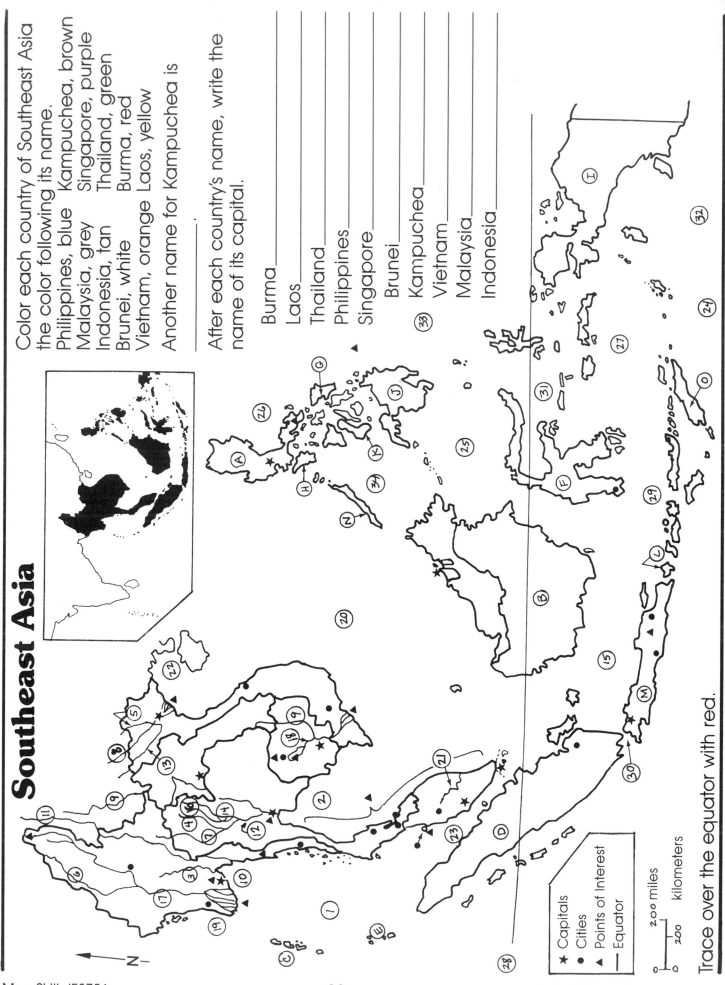

Capitals ★
Cities ●
Points of Interest ◀
Equator ——

200 miles
kilometers
200
0   0

Trace over the equator with red.

Southeast Asia (continued)

Locate the cities listed below. Write their letters below next to the symbols representing them on the map.

A. Da Nang
B. Mergui
C. Bangkok
D. Ipoh
E. Jakarta
F. Rangoon
G. Hat Yai

H. Ujung Pandang
I. Manila
J. George Town
K. Mandalay
L. Palembang
M. Kuala Lumpur

N. Bandar Seri Begawan
O. Nakhon Si Thammarat
P. Siem Reap
Q. Yogyakarta

R. Ho Chi Minh City (Saigon)
V. Hanoi
W. Songkhla
X. Bassein
Y. Surabaya
Z. Vientiane

Locate the following Points of Interest. Write their numbers below next to the symbols that represent them on the map.

1. Shwe Dagon Pagoda
2. Temple of the Emerald Buddha
3. Tenasserim Coast
4. Tonle Sap (Great Lake)
5. Mouths of the Mekong

6. Mouths of the Irrawaddy
7. Angkor Ruins
8. Red River Delta
9. Hkakabo Razi
10. Pinang Island

11. Malay Peninsula
12. Ancient Buddhist Kingdom: Borobudur
13. Philippine Trench
14. Mayon Volcano

Trace the rivers with blue. The rivers and some other bodies of water are numbered and circled on the map. Write their numbers on the map next to their names below.

___ Timor Sea
___ Molucca Sea
___ Salween River
___ Andaman Sea
___ Black River
___ Flores Sea
___ Red River
___ Wang River
___ China Sea

___ Gulf of Thailand
___ Banda Sea
___ Mekong River
___ Gulf of Martaban
___ Strait of Malacca
___ Southwest Pacific Ocean
___ Pahang River
___ Philippine Sea

___ Bay of Bengal
___ Sittang River
___ Chindwin River
___ Nan River
___ Yom River
___ Celebes Sea
___ Chao Phraya
___ Indian Ocean
___ Sunda Strait

___ Lo River
___ Java Sea
___ Sulu Sea
___ Ping River
___ Gulf of Tonkin
___ Irrawaddy River
     Arafura Sea
     Tonle Sap River

Which countries in this region are island countries?_____

Find out about how many islands there are in each country and write the number after the name of the country above.

Some of the islands on the map have a circled letter on them. Write the names of those islands following their correct letters below.

A._____ E._____ I. _____ M_____

B._____ F._____ J. _____ N_____

C._____ G._____ K. _____ O_____

D._____ H._____ L. _____

What two islands above actually do not belong to any of the countries of

Southeast Asia?_____

Japan and the Koreas

Japan is made up of four main islands—Hokkaido, Honshu, Shikoku, Kyushu—and thousands of smaller ones.

Color Honshu orange, Kyushu red, Hokkaido brown and Shikoku purple. Color North Korea grey and South Korea green.

There are bodies of water numbered and circled on the map. Write the name of each next to its number below.

1. _____   6. _____
2. _____   7. _____
3. _____   8. _____
4. _____   9. _____
5. _____

Locate the following cities. Write their letters next to the symbols representing them on the map.

A. Yokohama   D. Tokyo   G. Kyoto   J. Nagasaki
B. Seoul   E. Pyongyang   H. Nagoya   K. Pusan
C. Sapporo   F. Hiroshima   I. Osaka   L. Kaesong

Write the names of the capitals for the three countries below.

South Korea _____ Japan _____ North Korea _____

Locate the following Points of Interest. Write their numbers below next to the symbols representing them on the map.

1. Mount Fuji   5. The Imperial Palace   8. Ryukyu Islands   11. Halla-san
2. Kuril Islands   6. Tsushima Islands   9. Izu Islands   12. Seikan Tunnel
3. Cheju Island   7. Japanese Alps   10. Paektu-san
4. The Great Buddha

Color the National Parks green.

How would you describe this part of the world geographically? _____

Legend:
★ Capitals
● Cities
▲ Points of Interest
∧∧∧ Mountains
+ High Points
▨ National Parks

250 miles
250 kilometers
N

Facts About Eurasia

Eurasia is a name for _____.

Several "scrambled" capitals of Europe and Asia are in the box below.
Unscramble them and write them and their numbers next to their countries.

1. LOUSE	2. KNOBGKA	3. WOMCSO	4. SBLOIN	5. TRKJAAA	6. HOINA
7. HKCOOLTMS	8. IGNEBJI	9. NARHETE	10. THASEN	11. RIEBTU	12. BADGADH
13. AAANKR	14. MMATSREAD	15. ENW HILED	16. HNMPO PNHE	17. IMRDAD	
18. RAWWAS	19. NAVEIN	20. SAMDSAUC	21. SNIHLIEK	22. TUKIWA	
23. RGPAEU	24. LRBAGDEE	25. URLSEBSS	26. IETPAI	27. PNHCEENOGA	

Belgium_____   Thailand_____   Indonesia_____
South Korea_____   Portugal_____   Russia_____
Denmark_____   Vietnam_____   Kampuchea_____
Austria_____   Sweden_____   India_____
Finland_____   Lebanon_____   Netherlands_____
Kuwait_____   Syria_____   Iraq_____
Czechoslovakia_____   Iran_____   Spain_____
Yugoslavia_____   China_____   Poland_____
Greece_____   Turkey_____   Taiwan_____

Read the descriptions of several countries below. From each description write the name of the country.

This country is surrounded by Russia and China. It is _____.

This country is at the end of a peninsula in the Yellow Sea. It is _____.

This country is bordered by Spain to its southwest and by West Germany to its northeast. It is _____.

This country is on the mainland of Italy on the Adriatic Sea. It is _____.

This country is bounded by the Black Sea to the east, Romania to the north, Yugoslavia to the west and by Turkey and Greece to the south. It is _____.

This country is bordered by India to its south and west, China to the north and Sikkum to the east. It is _____.

This country is an island in the Indian Ocean. It is _____.

The Equator runs through this country. The country is _____.

This country is physically divided by the Sea of Marmara. It is _____.

This country is the largest country in the world. It is _____.

This country is a mountain country north and west of Italy, south of West Germany and east of France. It is _____.

Northern Africa

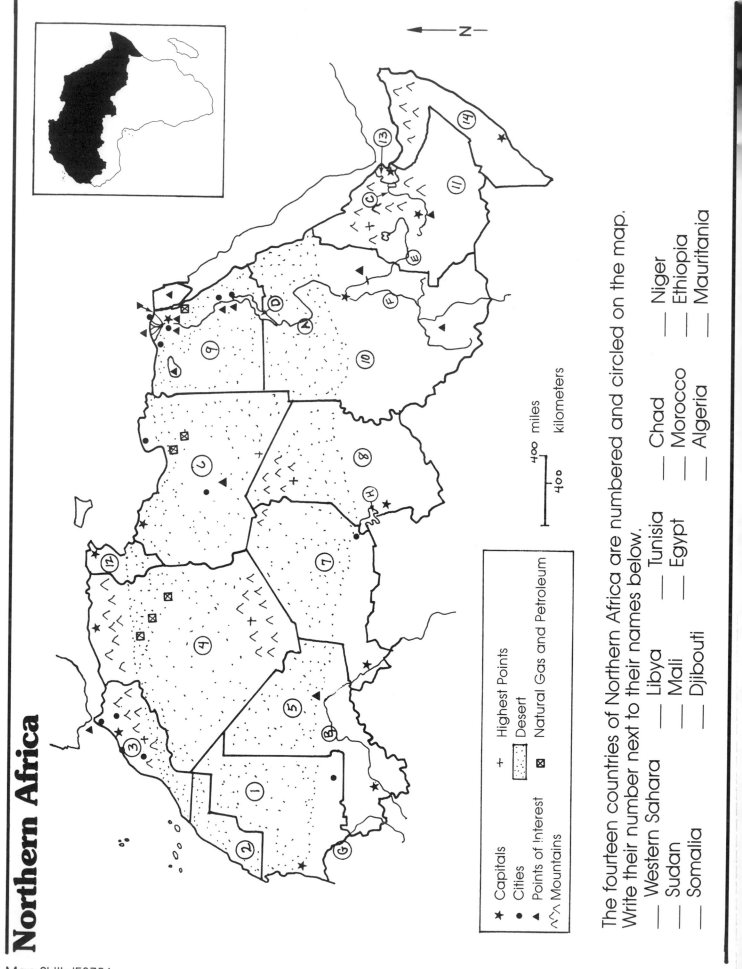

The fourteen countries of Northern Africa are numbered and circled on the map.
Write their number next to their names below.

___ Western Sahara   ___ Libya   ___ Tunisia   ___ Chad   ___ Niger
___ Sudan   ___ Mali   ___ Egypt   ___ Morocco   ___ Ethiopia
___ Somalia   ___ Djibouti   ___ Algeria   ___ Mauritania

Legend:
★ Capitals
● Cities
▲ Points of Interest
∧∧ Mountains
+ Highest Points
▦ Desert
⊠ Natural Gas and Petroleum

400 miles
400 kilometers

—N—

Northern Africa (continued)

Write the number of each country next to its capital below.

___ Cairo   ___ Tunis   ___ Niamey   ___ Khartoum
___ Rabat   ___ Bamako   ___ Mogadishu   ___ Addis Ababa
___ Nouakchott   ___ Algiers   ___ Tripoli   ___ Djibouti
___ N'Djamena

Which country does not have a capital?_____

Label the following places and bodies of water on the map.

Indian Ocean   Spain   Gulf of Sidra   Madeira Islands
Gulf of Aden   Sicily   Atlantic Ocean
Canary Islands   Red Sea   Mediterranean Sea

Circle the Atlas Mountains purple and the Ahaggar Mountains red. Color the Sahara Desert yellow. In how many countries does it reach? ___

Locate the following Points of Interest. Write their numbers below next to the symbols on the map that represent them.

1. Sinai Peninsula
2. Strait of Gibralter
3. Suez Canal
4. Niger Bend
5. Qattara Depression
6. Huge underground lake
7. Nile Delta
8. Sudd
9. Great Pyramids and the Sphinx
10. Valley of the Kings
11. Great Rift Valley
12. Aswan Dam
13. Sennar Dam
14. Ancient cities of Memphis and Saqqarah

Locate the following cities. Write their letters next to the dots that represent them on the map.

A. Némá
B. Casablanca
C. Marrakech
D. Nguigmi
E. Benghazi
F. Tangier
G. Alexandria
H. Al Fuqaha
I. Giza
J. Fez
K. Aswan
L. Luxor
M. Port Said

The following bodies of water have circled letters on them on the map. Trace over or color the bodies of water with blue and write the letters on the map next to their names below.

___ Awash River   ___ The Nile   ___ Sénégal River
___ Blue Nile   ___ Lake Nasser   ___ Niger River
___ White Nile   ___ Lake Chad

What countries are oil-producing countries?_____

To whom do the Canary Islands belong ?_____ Madeira Islands?_____

Name the countries and their Highest Points that are marked on the map.

_____

_____

West Africa

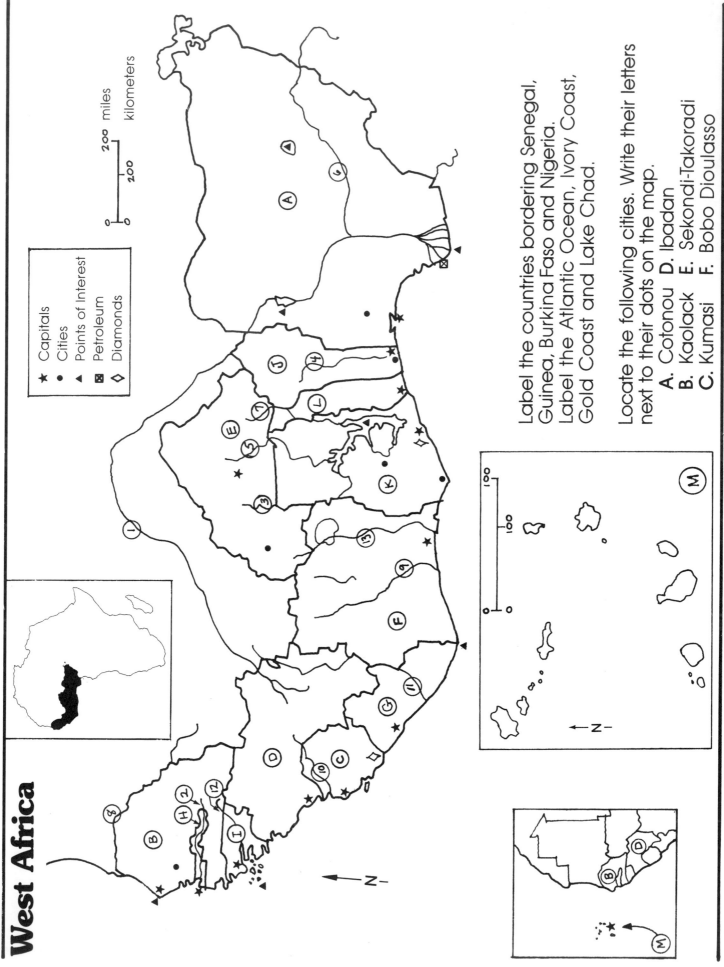

Capitals ★
Cities ●
Points of Interest ▲
Petroleum ⊠
Diamonds ◇

200 miles
200 kilometers

Label the countries bordering Senegal, Guinea, Burkina Faso and Nigeria.
Label the Atlantic Ocean, Ivory Coast, Gold Coast and Lake Chad.

Locate the following cities. Write their letters next to their dots on the map.
A. Cotonou D. Ibadan
B. Kaolack E. Sekondi-Takoradi
C. Kumasi F. Bobo Dioulasso

West Africa (continued)

Draw a line from the capital in the left column to its country in the middle column. Draw a line from each country's name in the middle column to the letter in the right column that matches the circled letter of the country on the map.

Banjul	Benin	H
Abidjan	Burkina Faso	J
Lagos	Gambia	K
Porto-Novo	Ghana	D
Accra	Guinea	I
Ougadougou	Guinea-Bissau	A
Lomé	Ivory Coast	G
Bissau	Cape Verde	E
Conakry	Liberia	M
Freetown	Nigeria	C
Dakar	Senegal	L
Praia	Sierra Leone	F
Monrovia	Togo	B

Locate the following Points of Interest. Write their numbers next to the symbols representing them on the map.

1. Cape Palmas
2. Lake Volta
3. Bijagós Islands
4. Niger Delta
5. Kainji Lake
6. Cape Verde
7. Yankari Game Reserve

The rivers have a circled number on them. Trace over the rivers on the map with blue. Write the names of the rivers next to their numbers below.

1. _____
2. _____
3. _____
4. _____
5. _____

6. _____
7. _____
8. _____
9. _____

10. _____
11. _____
12. _____
13. _____

Where does the Niger River begin? _____

Which country produces petroleum? _____ Which countries mine diamonds? _____

What is the westernmost point of Africa? _____

West Central Africa

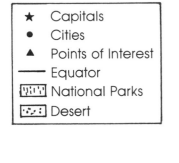

★ Capitals
● Cities
▲ Points of Interest
── Equator
National Parks
Desert

0   100   300   miles
0   100   300   kilometers

N

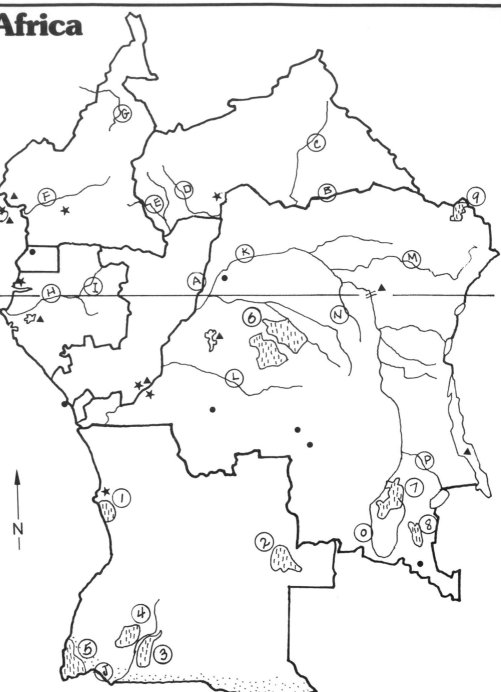

Color the countries of West Central Africa the color following their names in parentheses. Write the name of each country's capital on the line following its name.

Central African Republic (blue)_____

Equatorial Guinea (grey)_____ Congo (purple)_____

Zaire (yellow)_____ Gabon (green)_____

Cameroon (orange)_____ Angola (red)_____

São Tomé and Príncipe (circle brown)_____

West Central Africa (continued)

The following national parks are numbered in circles on the map. Write the number of each national park next to its name below.

___ Kundelungu   ___ Mupa   ___ Salonga
___ Garamba   ___ Quicama   ___ Cameia
___ Bikuar   ___ Upemba   ___ Porto Alexandre

Several rivers are marked with a circled letter. Write the name of each river next to its letter below.

A. _____   G. _____   L. _____
B. _____   H. _____   M. _____
C. _____   I. _____   N. _____
D. _____   J. _____   O. _____
E. _____   K. _____   P. _____
F. _____

Where does the Congo start?_____

_____

Where does it end?_____

Name three of its tributaries._____

Label the Atlantic Ocean and the Gulf of Guinea.

Equatorial Guinea

Label the following cities next to the symbols that represent them.

Kananga   Pointe-Noire   Kikwit
Mbuji-Mayi   Bata
Lubumbashi   Mbandaka

Locate the following Points of Interest. Write their numbers below next to the symbols representing them on the map.

1. Stanley Falls   **5.** Mt. Cameroon
2. Lake Onangué   **6.** Lake Mai-Ndombe
3. Lake Tanganyika   **7.** Stanley Pool
4. Fernando Po

What are the names of the territories of Equatorial Guinea?

1. _____   3. _____   5. _____
2. _____   4. _____

Which is the mainland?_____

On which is the capital?_____

East Central Africa

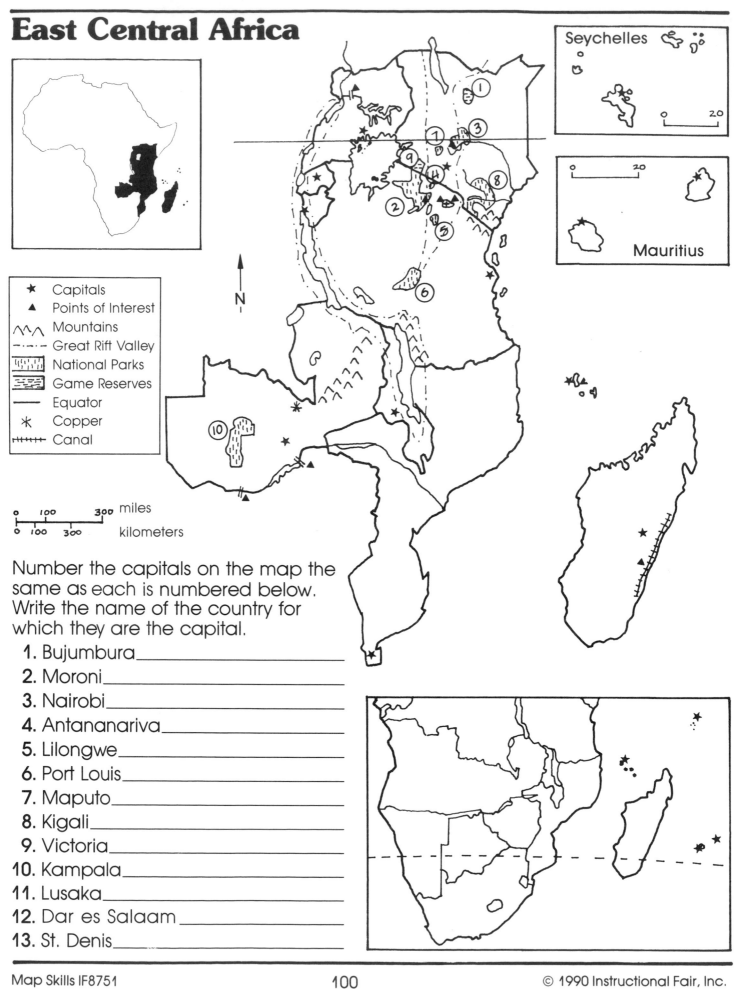

Seychelles

Mauritius

Legend:
- ★ Capitals
- ▲ Points of Interest
- ∧∧∧ Mountains
- -·-·- Great Rift Valley
- National Parks
- Game Reserves
- — Equator
- ✳ Copper
- ++++ Canal

N

miles
kilometers

Number the capitals on the map the same as each is numbered below. Write the name of the country for which they are the capital.

1. Bujumbura_____
2. Moroni_____
3. Nairobi_____
4. Antananariva_____
5. Lilongwe_____
6. Port Louis_____
7. Maputo_____
8. Kigali_____
9. Victoria_____
10. Kampala_____
11. Lusaka_____
12. Dar es Salaam_____
13. St. Denis_____

East Central Africa (continued)

Name the island countries._____

Which country is an island but under the jurisdiction of France?_____

Which country is on the mainland but has islands too?_____

What is the mainland called?_____ the islands?_____

Trace over the Equator with red. Over what countries does it extend?_____

Trace the Great Rift Valley with yellow. What countries does it reach?_____

_____

The national parks and game reserves are numbered and circled on the map. Color the national parks green and the game reserves orange. Write the name of each below next to its number.

1. _____   6. _____
2. _____   7. _____
3. _____   8. _____
4. _____   9. _____
5. _____   10. _____

Trace or color the following bodies of water blue. Write their letters below on the map where they are located.

   A. Zambezi River   F. Lake Nyasa   J. Lake Kivu
   B. Lake Turkana   G. Albert Nile   K. Lake Victoria
   C. Tana River   H. Athi River   L. Lake Kyoga
   D. Lake Tanganyika   I. Kariba Lake   M. Victoria Nile
   E. Lake Albert

What countries bound Lake Victoria?_____

Where does the Zambezi River begin?_____   _____

Where does it flow?_____

_____

Where does it end?_____

Label the following physical geographic features.

   Muchinga Mountains   Indian Ocean   Usambara Mountains
   Mozambique Channel   Livingstone Mountains   Zanzibar Channel

Locate the following Points of Interest. Write the numbers below next to the symbols representing them on the map.

   14. Victoria Falls   17. Mont Kartala   20. Meru Crater
   15. Pangalanes Canal   18. Ngorongoro Crater   21. Murchison Falls
   16. Mt. Kenya   19. Kariba Dam   22. Kilimanjaro

What country is a large producer of copper?_____

Southern Africa

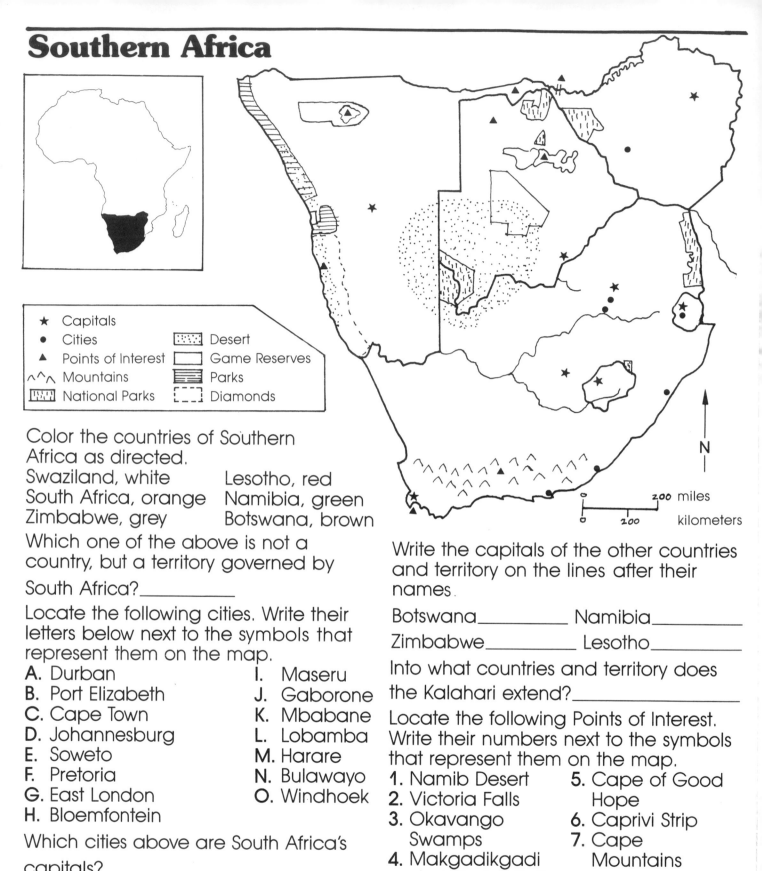

Color the countries of Southern
Africa as directed.

Swaziland, white   Lesotho, red
South Africa, orange   Namibia, green
Zimbabwe, grey   Botswana, brown

Which one of the above is not a
country, but a territory governed by

South Africa?_____

Locate the following cities. Write their
letters below next to the symbols that
represent them on the map.

A. Durban   I. Maseru
B. Port Elizabeth   J. Gaborone
C. Cape Town   K. Mbabane
D. Johannesburg   L. Lobamba
E. Soweto   M. Harare
F. Pretoria   N. Bulawayo
G. East London   O. Windhoek
H. Bloemfontein

Which cities above are South Africa's

capitals?_____

Swaziland's?_____

Write the capitals of the other countries
and territory on the lines after their
names.

Botswana_____ Namibia_____

Zimbabwe_____ Lesotho_____

Into what countries and territory does

the Kalahari extend?_____

Locate the following Points of Interest.
Write their numbers next to the symbols
that represent them on the map.

1. Namib Desert   5. Cape of Good
2. Victoria Falls   Hope
3. Okavango   6. Caprivi Strip
   Swamps   7. Cape
4. Makgadikgadi   Mountains
   and Etosha Salt
   Pans

Circle the national parks black, game reserves purple and parks brown. Color
Kariba Lake blue. Trace the Limpopo, Orange and Vaal Rivers blue.
Label the oceans on the east and west sides of South Africa.

Answer Key

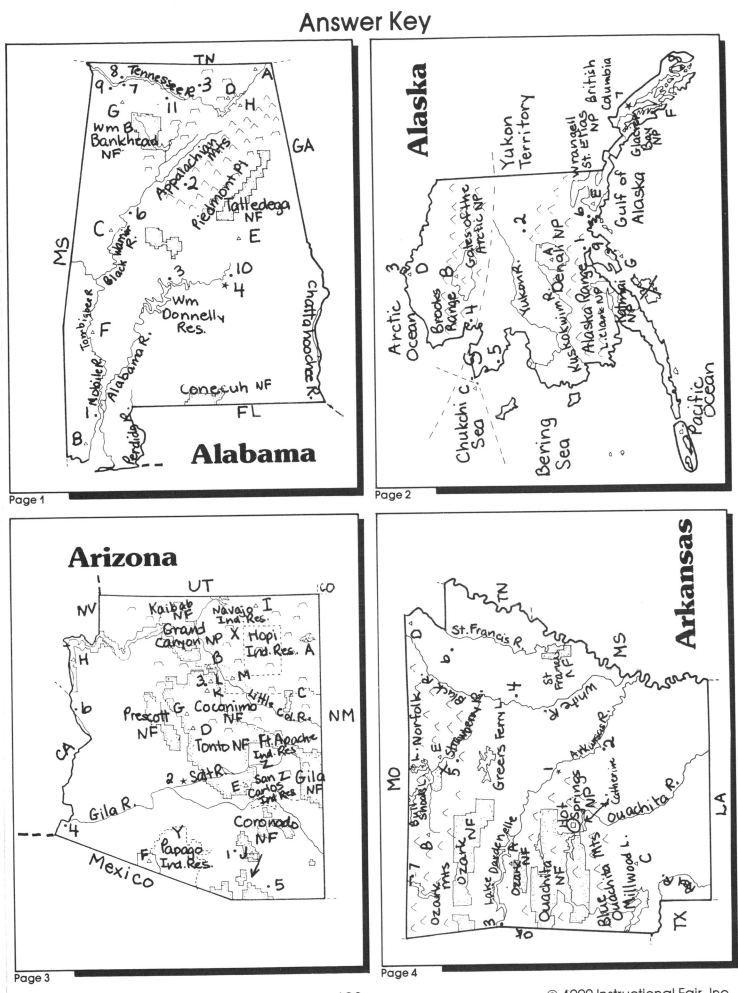

Page 1

Page 2

Page 3

Page 4

Map Skills IF8751

103

© 1990 Instructional Fair, Inc.

Answer Key

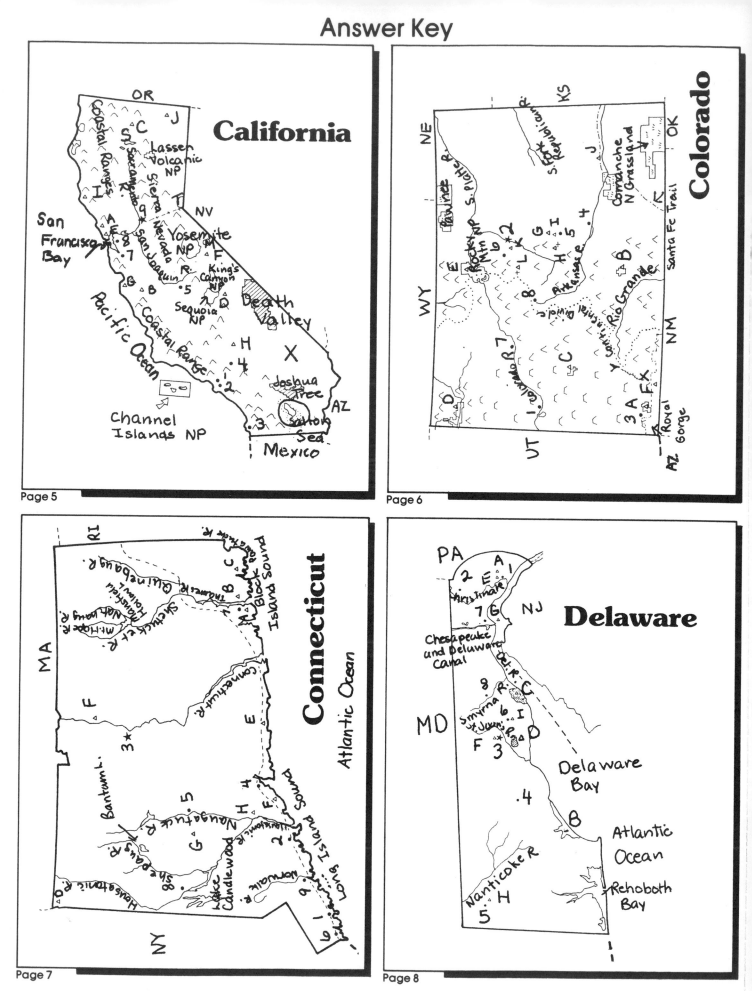

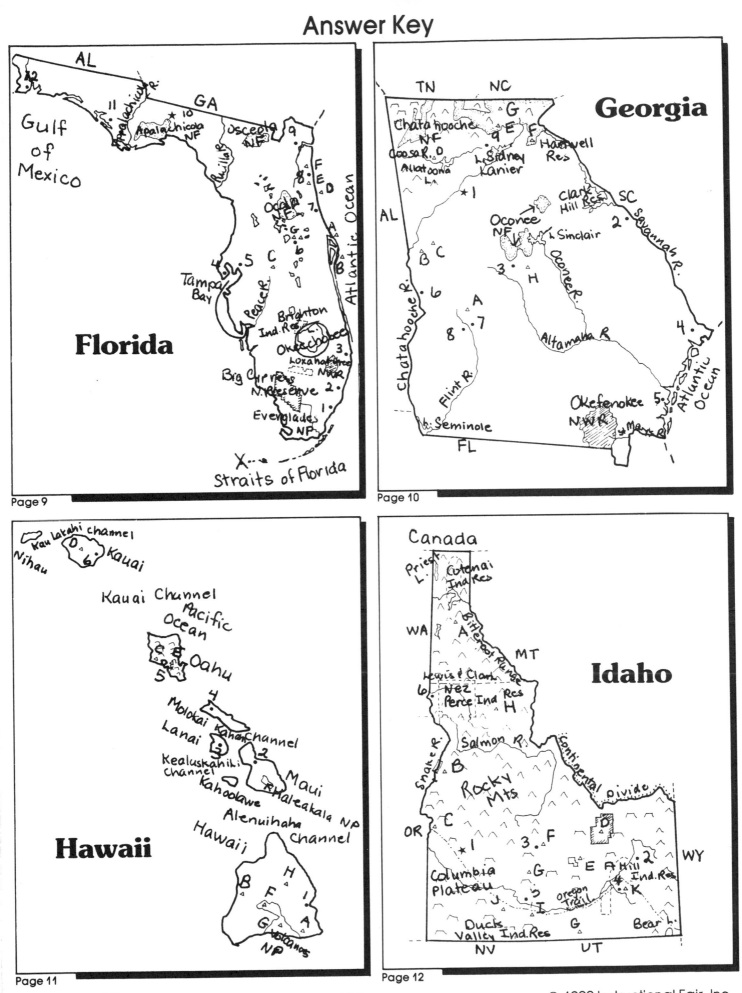

Florida

Gulf of Mexico

Georgia

Hawaii

Idaho

Page 9

Page 10

Page 11

Page 12

Answer Key

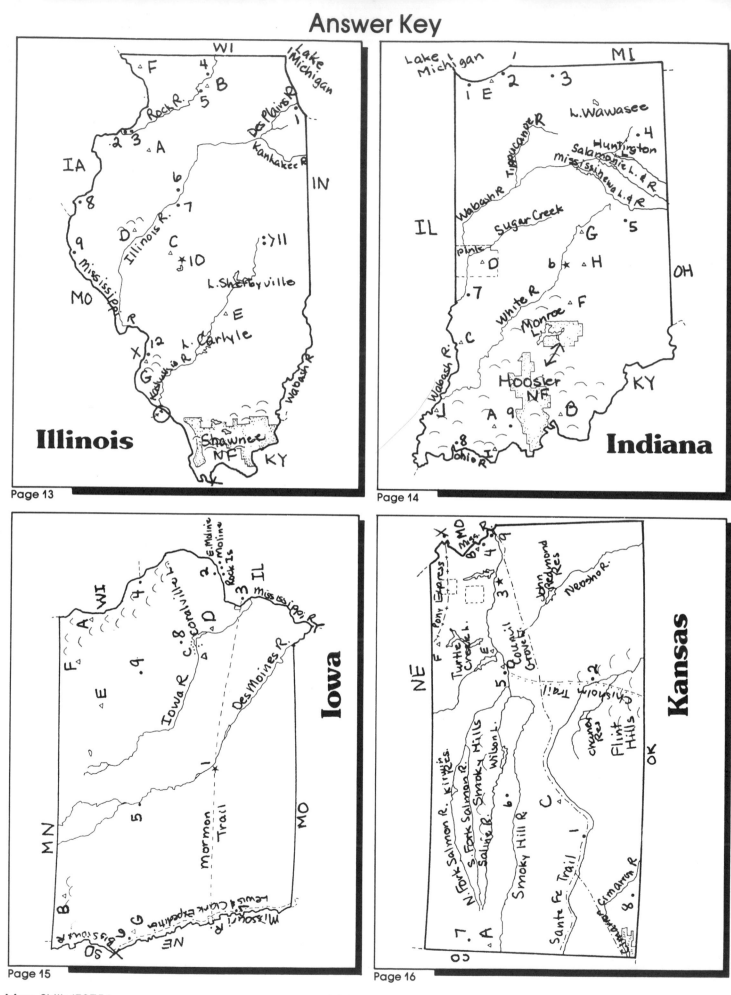

Illinois

Page 13

Indiana

Page 14

Iowa

Page 15

Kansas

Page 16

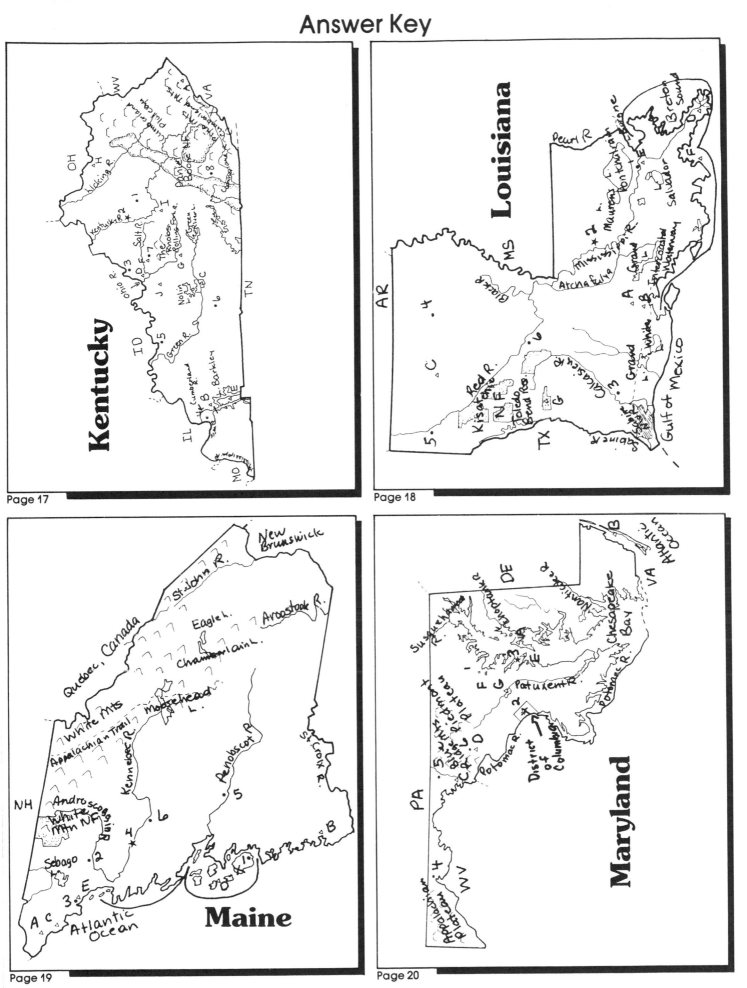

Page 17

Page 18

Page 19

Page 20

107

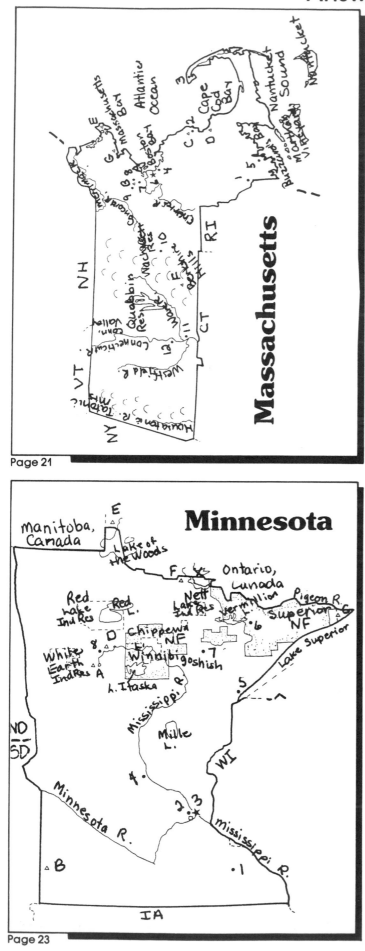

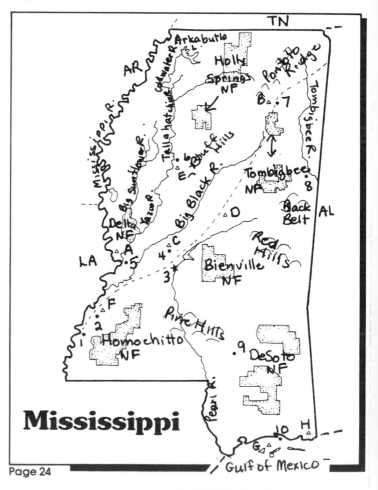

Massachusetts

Atlantic Ocean

Massachusetts Bay

Nantucket Sound

Cape Cod Bay

Boston Bay

Buzzards Bay

Vineyard

NH

VT

NY

CT

RI

MA

Quabbin Res.

Wachusett Res.

Connecticut R.

Westfield R.

Housatonic R.

Taconic Mts.

Conn. Valley

Chicopee R.

Merrimack R.

Michigan

Copper Range

Lake Superior

Ottawa NF

Menominee Mts.

Hiawatha NF

Lake Michigan

Soo Canal

Houghton L.

Huron NF

Manistee NF

Saginaw Bay

Lake Huron

Grand R.

Kalamazoo

Lake Erie

Lake Ontario

WI

ID

OH

Minnesota

Manitoba, Canada

Lake of the Woods

Ontario, Canada

Red Lake Ind Res

Red L.

Nett Lake Ind Res

Vermillion R.

Pigeon R.

Superior NF

Chippewa NF

Winnibigoshish

L. Itaska

White Earth Ind Res

Mississippi R.

Mille L.

Lake Superior

Minnesota R.

Mississippi R.

ND

SD

WI

IA

Mississippi

TN

Arkabutla L.

Holly Springs NF

Pontotoc Ridge

Tombigbee R.

Coldwater R.

Tallahatchie R.

Bluff Hills

Tombigbee NF

Black Belt

AR

Mississippi R.

Big Sunflower R.

Yazoo R.

Big Black R.

Red Hills

Delta NF

Bienville NF

Rice Hills

DeSoto NF

Homochitto NF

Pearl R.

LA

AL

Gulf of Mexico

Page 21

Page 22

Page 23

Page 24

Map Skills IF8751

108

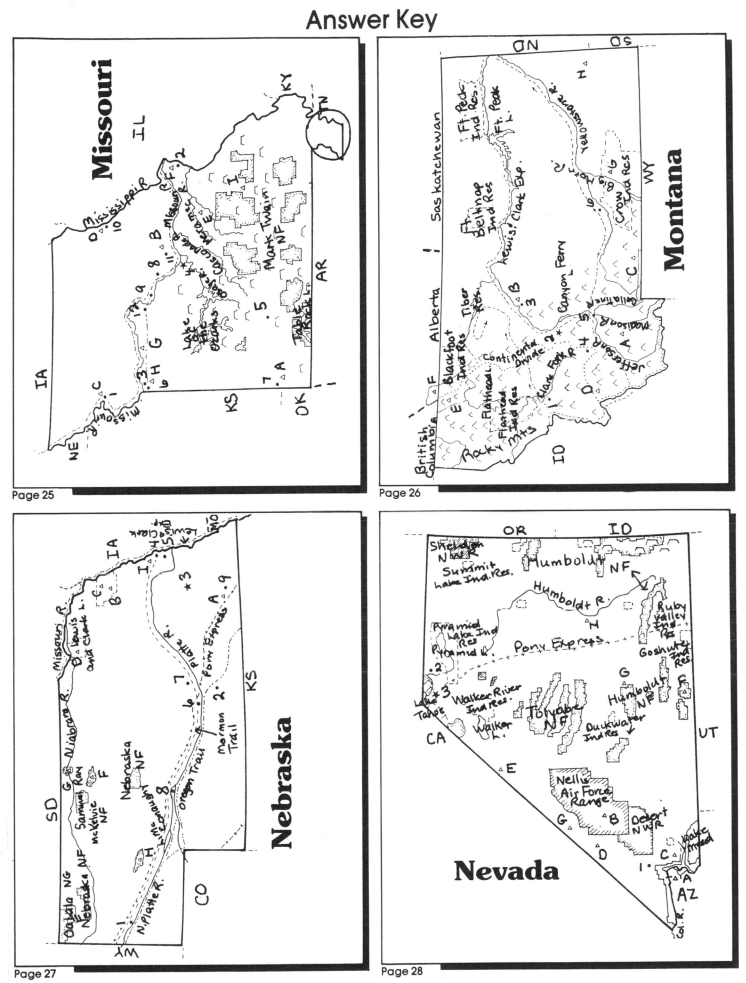

Page 25

Page 26

Page 27

Page 28

Map Skills IF8751

109

© 1990 Instructional Fair, Inc.

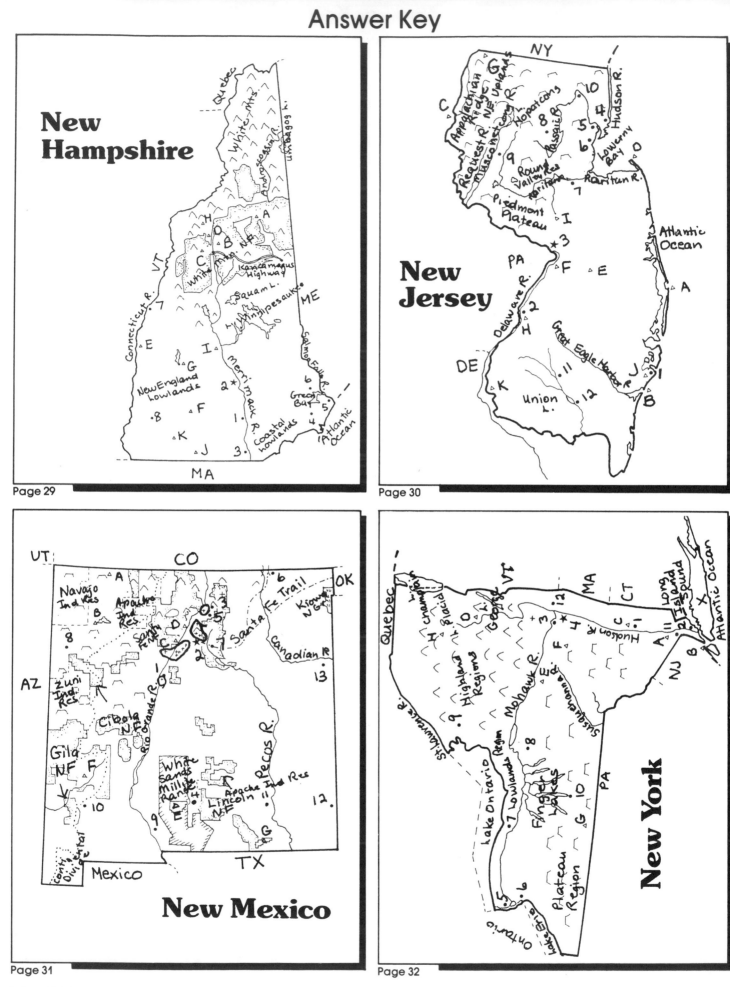

New Hampshire

Page 29

New Jersey

Page 30

New Mexico

Page 31

New York

Page 32

Answer Key

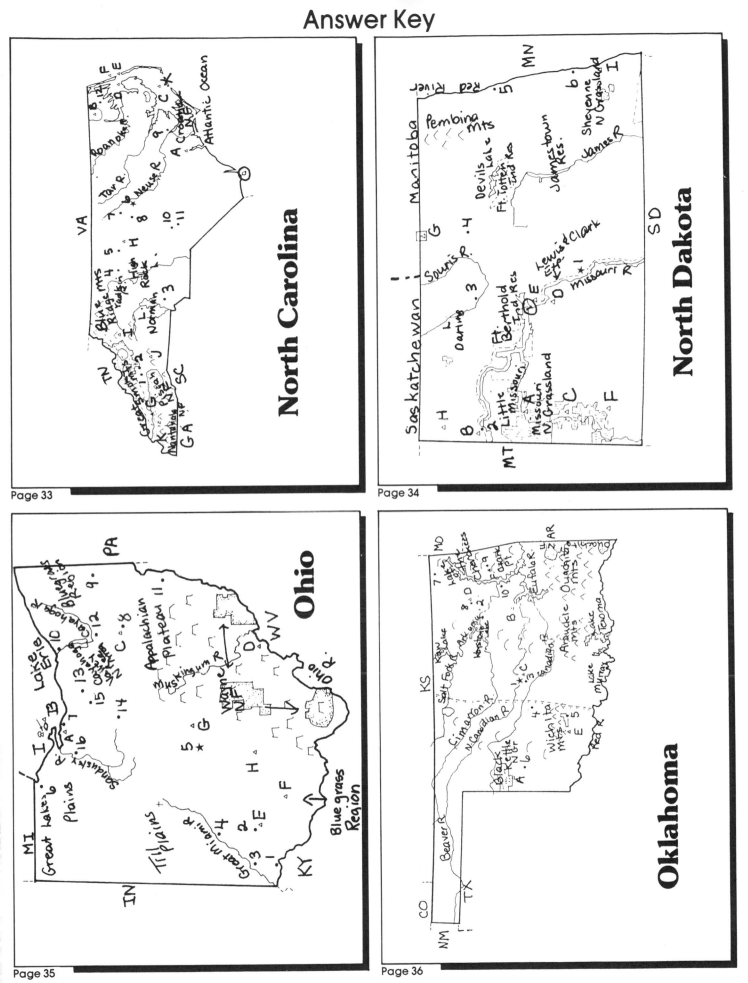

North Carolina — Page 33

North Dakota — Page 34

Ohio — Page 35

Oklahoma — Page 36

Page 33

Page 34

Page 35

Page 36

Map Skills IF8751

111

© 1990 Instructional Fair, Inc.

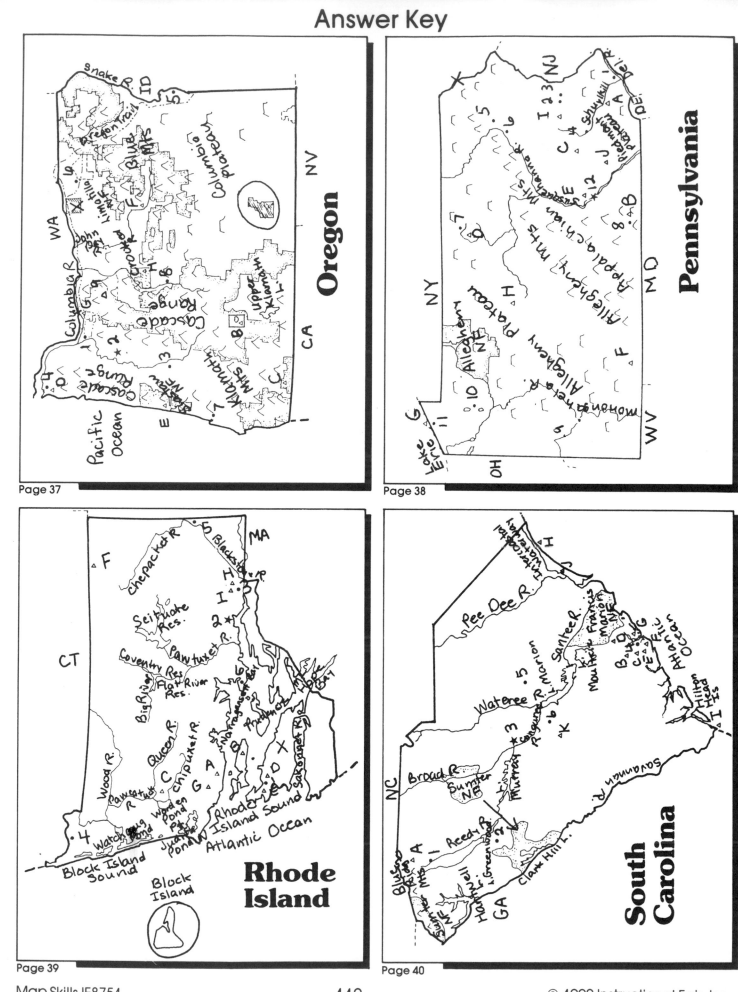

Page 37

Oregon

Page 38

Pennsylvania

Page 39

Rhode Island

Page 40

South Carolina

© 1990 Instructional Fair, Inc.

Answer Key

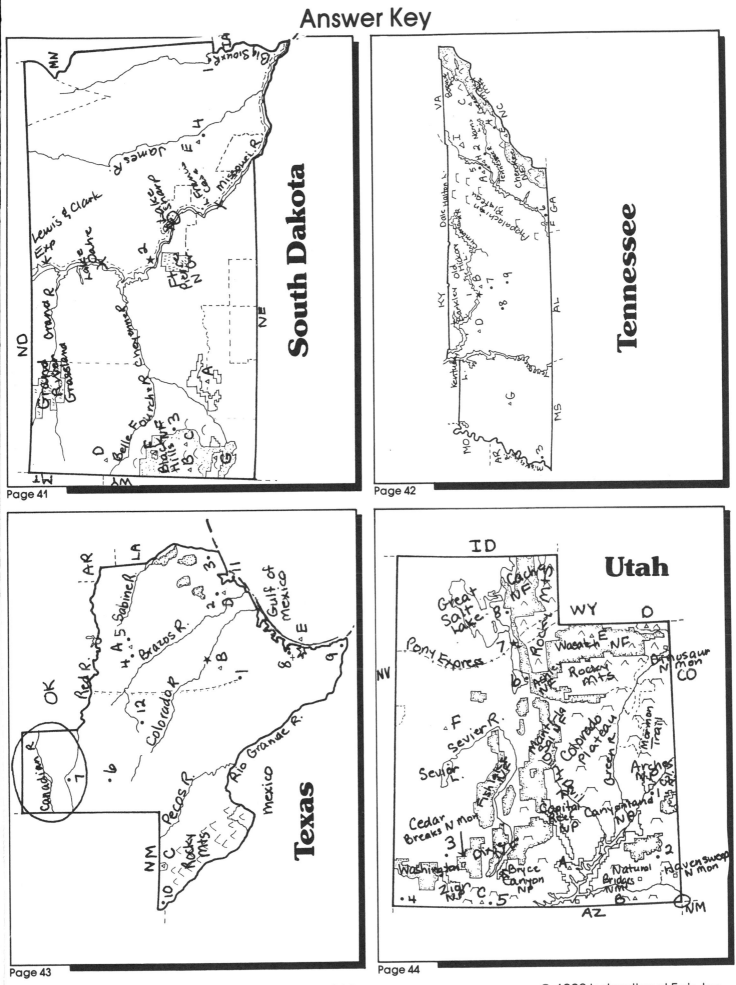

Page 41 — South Dakota

Page 42 — Tennessee

Page 43 — Texas

Page 44 — Utah

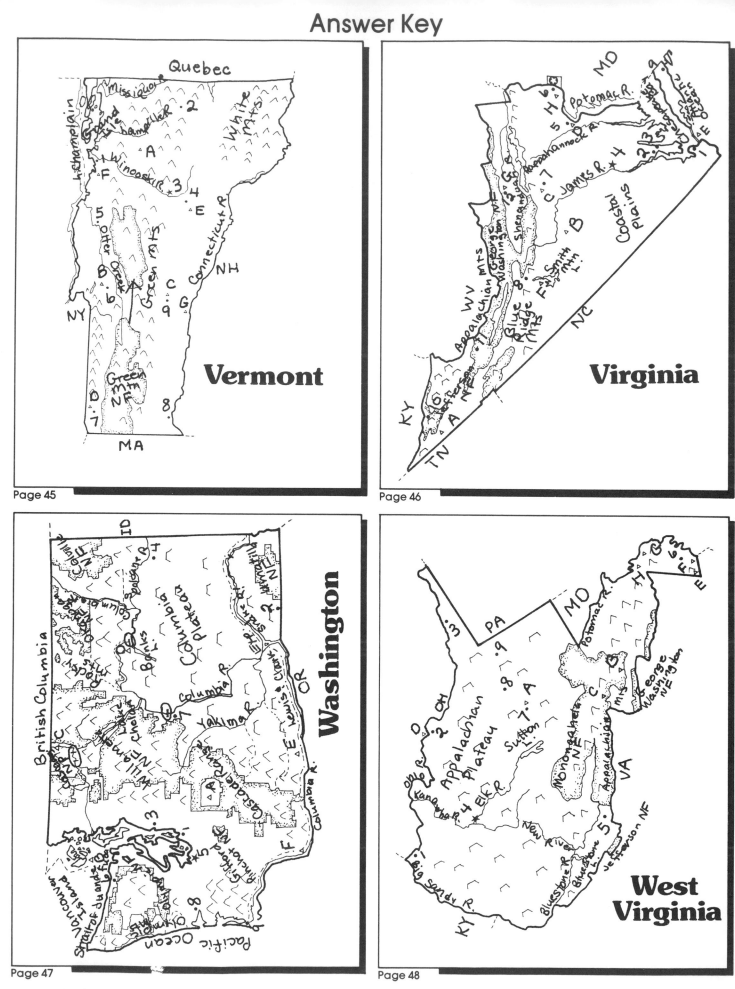

Vermont

Page 45

Virginia

Page 46

Washington

Page 47

West Virginia

Page 48

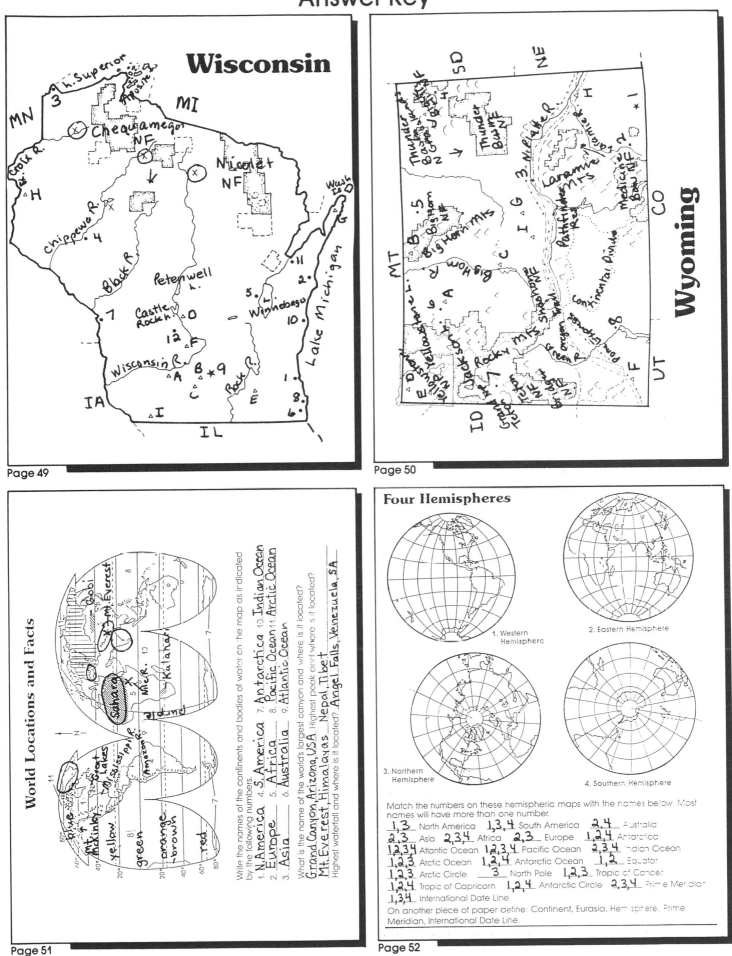

Wisconsin

Page 49

Wyoming

Page 50

World Locations and Facts

Write the names of the continents and bodies of water on the map as indicated by the following numbers.

1. N. America
2. Europe
3. Asia
4. S. America
5. Africa
6. Australia
7. Antarctica
8. Pacific Ocean
9. Atlantic Ocean
10. Indian Ocean
11. Arctic Ocean

What is the name of the world's largest canyon and where is it located?
Grand Canyon, Arizona, USA
Highest peak and where is it located?
Mt. Everest, Himalayas, Nepal, Tibet
Highest waterfall and where is it located? Angel Falls, Venezuela, SA

Page 51

Four Hemispheres

1. Western Hemisphere
2. Eastern Hemisphere
3. Northern Hemisphere
4. Southern Hemisphere

Match the numbers on these hemispheric maps with the names below. Most names will have more than one number.

1,3 North America	1,3,4 South America	2,4 Australia
2,3 Asia	2,3,4 Africa	2,3 Europe	1,2,4 Antarctica
1,2,3,4 Atlantic Ocean	1,2,3,4 Pacific Ocean	2,3,4 Indian Ocean
1,2,3 Arctic Ocean	1,2,4 Antarctic Ocean	1,2 Equator
1,2,3 Arctic Circle	3 North Pole	1,2,3 Tropic of Cancer
1,2,4 Tropic of Capricorn	1,2,4 Antarctic Circle	2,3,4 Prime Meridian
1,3,4 International Date Line		

On another piece of paper define: Continent, Eurasia, Hemisphere, Prime Meridian, International Date Line.

Page 52

Answer Key

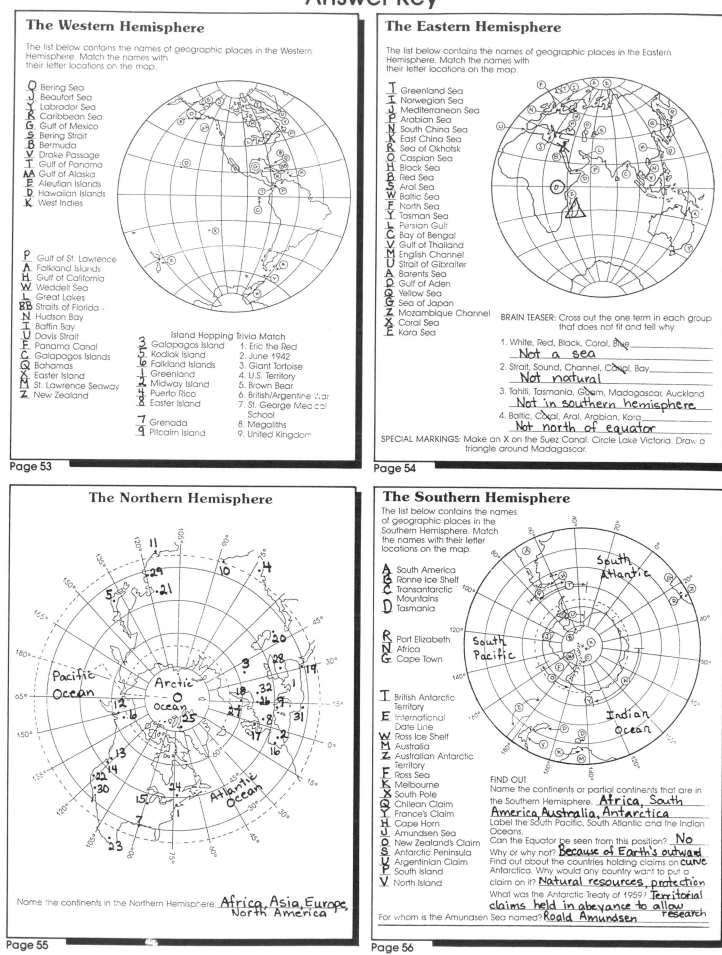

The Western Hemisphere

The list below contains the names of geographic places in the Western Hemisphere. Match the names with their letter locations on the map.

O Bering Sea
J Beaufort Sea
Y Labrador Sea
R Caribbean Sea
G Gulf of Mexico
S Bering Strait
B Bermuda
V Drake Passage
T Gulf of Panama
AA Gulf of Alaska
E Aleutian Islands
D Hawaiian Islands
K West Indies

P Gulf of St. Lawrence
A Falkland Islands
H Gulf of California
W Weddell Sea
L Great Lakes
BB Straits of Florida
N Hudson Bay
I Baffin Bay
U Davis Strait
F Panama Canal
C Galapagos Islands
Q Bahamas
X Easter Island
M St. Lawrence Seaway
Z New Zealand

Island Hopping Trivia Match

3 Galapagos Island
5 Kodiak Island
6 Falkland Islands
1 Greenland
2 Midway Island
4 Puerto Rico
8 Easter Island
7 Grenada
9 Pitcairn Island

1. Eric the Red
2. June 1942
3. Giant Tortoise
4. U.S. Territory
5. Brown Bear
6. British/Argentine War
7. St. George Medical School
8. Megaliths
9. United Kingdom

Page 53

The Eastern Hemisphere

The list below contains the names of geographic places in the Eastern Hemisphere. Match the names with their letter locations on the map.

I Greenland Sea
T Norwegian Sea
J Mediterranean Sea
P Arabian Sea
N South China Sea
K East China Sea
R Sea of Okhotsk
O Caspian Sea
H Black Sea
B Red Sea
S Aral Sea
W Baltic Sea
F North Sea
Y Tasman Sea
L Persian Gulf
C Bay of Bengal
V Gulf of Thailand
M English Channel
U Strait of Gibralter
A Barents Sea
D Gulf of Aden
Q Yellow Sea
G Sea of Japan
Z Mozambique Channel
X Coral Sea
E Kara Sea

BRAIN TEASER: Cross out the one term in each group that does not fit and tell why.

1. White, Red, Black, Coral, Blue
   Not a sea

2. Strait, Sound, Channel, Canal, Bay
   Not natural

3. Tahiti, Tasmania, Guam, Madagascar, Auckland
   Not in southern hemisphere

4. Baltic, Coral, Aral, Arabian, Kara
   Not north of equator

SPECIAL MARKINGS: Make an X on the Suez Canal. Circle Lake Victoria. Draw a triangle around Madagascar.

Page 54

The Northern Hemisphere

Name the continents in the Northern Hemisphere. Africa, Asia, Europe, North America

Page 55

The Southern Hemisphere

The list below contains the names of geographic places in the Southern Hemisphere. Match the names with their letter locations on the map.

A South America
B Ronne Ice Shelf
C Transantarctic Mountains
D Tasmania

R Port Elizabeth
N Africa
G Cape Town

I British Antarctic Territory
E International Date Line
W Ross Ice Shelf
M Australia
Z Australian Antarctic Territory
F Ross Sea
K Melbourne
X South Pole
Q Chilean Claim
Y France's Claim
H Cape Horn
J Amundsen Sea
O New Zealand's Claim
S Antarctic Peninsula
U Argentinian Claim
P South Island
V North Island

FIND OUT
Name the continents or partial continents that are in the Southern Hemisphere. Africa, South America Australia, Antarctica
Label the South Pacific, South Atlantic and the Indian Oceans.
Can the Equator be seen from this position? No
Why or why not? Because of Earth's outward curve
Find out about the countries holding claims on Antarctica. Why would any country want to put a claim on it? Natural resources, protection
What was the Antarctic Treaty of 1959? Territorial claims held in abeyance to allow research
For whom is the Amundsen Sea named? Roald Amundsen

Page 56

Map Skills IF8751

116

© 1990 Instructional Fair, Inc.

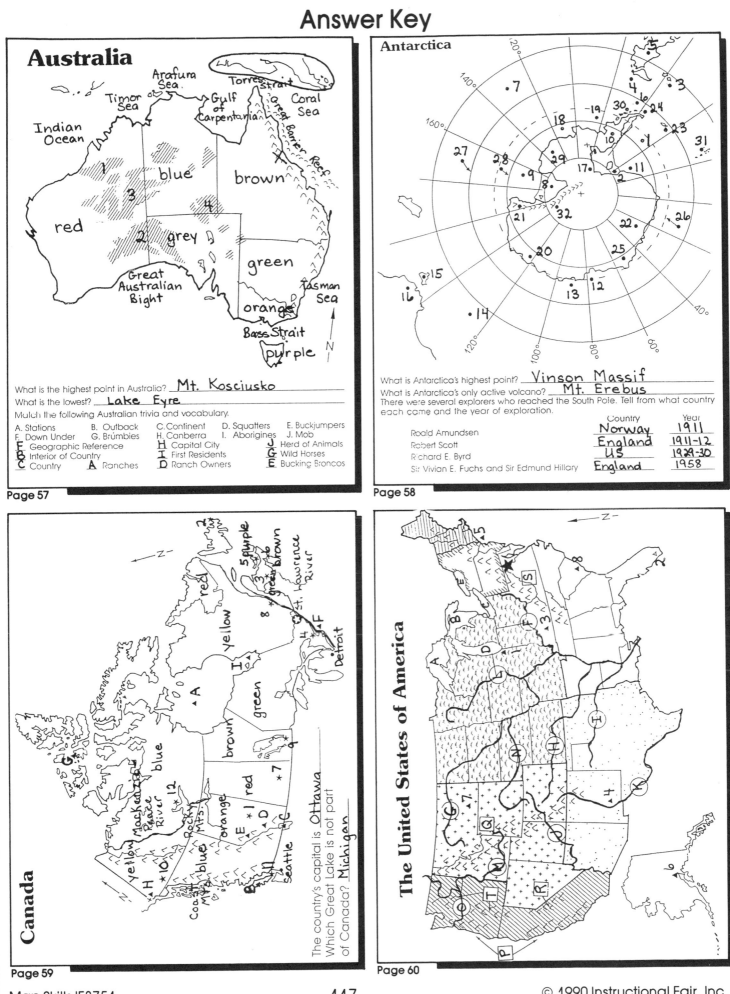

Australia

Arafura Sea
Timor Sea
Gulf of Carpentaria
Torres Strait
Coral Sea
Great Barrier Reef
Indian Ocean
blue
brown
red
3
grey
4
green
Great Australian Bight
Tasman Sea
orange
Bass Strait
purple
N

What is the highest point in Australia? **Mt. Kosciusko**
What is the lowest? **Lake Eyre**

Match the following Australian trivia and vocabulary.

A. Stations	B. Outback	C. Continent	D. Squatters	E. Buckjumpers
F. Down Under	G. Brumbies	H. Canberra	I. Aborigines	J. Mob
F Geographic Reference		**H** Capital City		**J** Herd of Animals
B Interior of Country		**I** First Residents		**G** Wild Horses
C Country	**A** Ranches	**D** Ranch Owners		**E** Bucking Broncos

Page 57

Antarctica

.7
.20°
140°
.4
.5
.3
-19
30
6
.24
160°
18
10
.Y
.23
31
27
28
29
+
17
.2
.11
.9
8
+
21
32
22.
.26
.20
25
.15
.13
.12
II.
.14
120°
100°
80°
60°
40°

What is Antarctica's highest point? **Vinson Massif**
What is Antarctica's only active volcano? **Mt. Erebus**
There were several explorers who reached the South Pole. Tell from what country each came and the year of exploration.

	Country	Year
Roald Amundsen	Norway	1911
Robert Scott	England	1911-12
Richard E. Byrd	US	1929-30
Sir Vivian E. Fuchs and Sir Edmund Hillary	England	1958

Page 58

Canada

2
5 purple
3
grey
brown
St. Lawrence River
red
Yellow
I
8
A
4
F
Detroit
green
brown
G
blue
Mackenzie
Peace River
12
6
red
7
orange
E
D
C
B
Seattle
Coast Mts.
Rocky Mts.
blue
H
10
N

The country's capital is **Ottawa**
Which Great Lake is not part of Canada? **Michigan**

Page 59

The United States of America

N
5
S
8
2
F
3
B
C
E
D
I
A
H
W
H
K
G
7
Q
4
M
O
T
R
6
P

Page 60

Answer Key

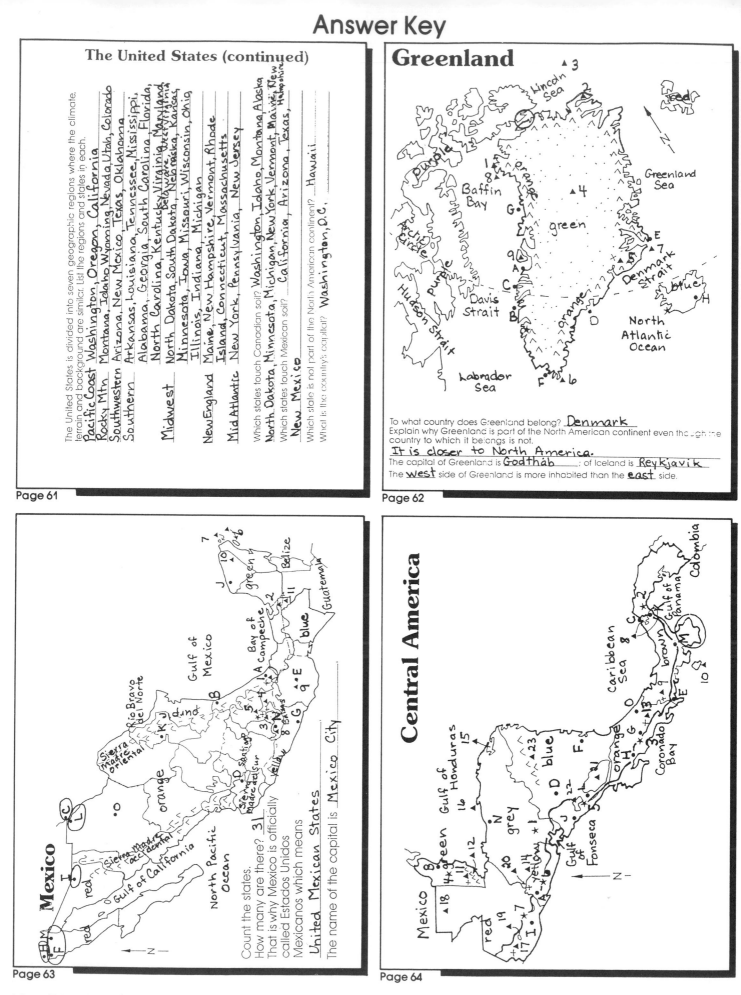

The United States (continued)

The United States is divided into seven geographic regions where the climate, terrain and background are similar. List the regions and states in each.

Pacific Coast — Washington, Oregon, California
Rocky Mtn — Montana, Idaho, Wyoming, Nevada, Utah, Colorado
Southwestern — Arizona, New Mexico, Texas, Oklahoma
Southern — Arkansas, Louisiana, Tennessee, Mississippi, Alabama, Georgia, South Carolina, Florida, North Carolina, Kentucky, Virginia, West Virginia, Maryland, Delaware
Midwest — North Dakota, South Dakota, Nebraska, Kansas, Minnesota, Iowa, Missouri, Wisconsin, Ohio, Illinois, Indiana, Michigan
New England — Maine, New Hampshire, Vermont, Rhode Island, Connecticut, Massachusetts
Mid Atlantic — New York, Pennsylvania, New Jersey

Which states touch Canadian soil? Washington, Idaho, Montana, Alaska, North Dakota, Minnesota, Michigan, New York, Vermont, Maine, New Hampshire
Which states touch Mexican soil? California, Arizona, Texas, New Mexico

Which state is not part of the North American continent? Hawaii
What is the country's capital? Washington, D.C.

Page 61

Greenland

To what country does Greenland belong? Denmark
Explain why Greenland is part of the North American continent even though the country to which it belongs is not.
It is closer to North America.
The capital of Greenland is Godthåb ; of Iceland is Reykjavik
The west side of Greenland is more inhabited than the east side.

Page 62

Mexico

Count the states.
How many are there? 31
That is why Mexico is officially called Estados Unidos Mexicanos which means
United Mexican States
The name of the capital is Mexico City

Page 63

Central America

Page 64

Answer Key

The Panama Canal

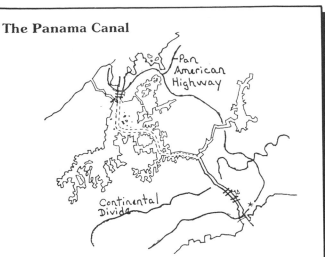

A ship on the Atlantic Ocean enters the Panama Canal at the city of **Colón** by way of **Limón Bay** which is the harbor for the town of **Cristóbal**. The ship travels through the bay to the **Gatun Locks**. There, three locks raise the ship to the level of **Gatun Lake**. The ship then sails past the **Gatun Dam** that holds back the Chagres River, across the lake to **Gamboa**. Here the ship enters the eight mile, man-made **Gaillard Cut** that goes between **Gold Hill** on the east and **Contractor's Hill** on the west. When the ship is at the end of the cut it enters the **Pedro Miguel Locks** which lower it to **Miraflores Lake**. The ship then travels across to the **Miraflores Locks** which lower it to the level of the Pacific Ocean. Before it reaches the Pacific, the ship passes under the **Thatcher Ferry** Bridge and into the **Bay of Panama**.
A ship going from the Atlantic Ocean to the Pacific travels from a **northwest** direction into a **southeast** one.

Page 65

West Indies

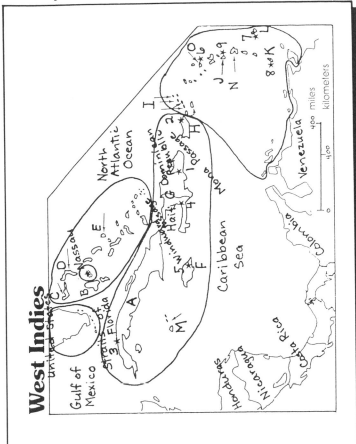

Page 66

Facts About North America

Draw a line from the number on the left to the fact it tells about on the right.

7,071,000 — Distance in miles of Panama Canal
12,000 — Year Panama Canal was built
49 — Number of states in U.S. on the North American continent
10 — Highest waterfall in North America, Yosemite Falls
7 — Approximate number of ships that pass through the Panama Canal in a year
440 — North America's largest city, New York
50,72 — Number of states in Central America
1999 — Years it took to build the Panama Canal
11 — Percent of land covered by ice in Greenland
20,320 — Year Panama will take over the management of the Panama Canal
1914 — Feet below sea level of North America's lowest point, Death Valley
1,071 — Number of countries in North America
80 — Highest point in North America, Mt. McKinley
31,700 — Square miles of North America's largest lake, Superior
282 — Miles northernmost Greenland is from North Pole
2,425 — Miles of North America's longest river, Mackenzie

Classify the places named in the box below. Write their names after the type of feature that is listed below the box.

Chihuahuan	Rio Grande	Cuba	Cascade	Mojave	White
Greenland	Arkansas	Aleutians	Michigan	Sonoran
Okeechobee	Bermuda	Sierra Madre	Mackenzie	St. Lawrence

ISLANDS **Greenland, Bermuda, Cuba, Aleutians**
LAKES **Michigan, Okeechobee**
RIVERS **Rio Grande, Mackenzie, St. Lawrence, Arkansas, White**
MOUNTAIN RANGES **Cascade, Sierra Madre**
DESERTS **Chihuahuan, Mojave, Sonoran**
If you were a bird and could fly a direct route from each of the following, over what countries would you fly?
1. Mexico City to Quebec **Mexico, United States, Canada**
2. Salt Lake City to Virginia Beach **United States**
3. Toronto to Anchorage **Canada, United States**
4. New York to Cristóbal Colón **U.S., Cuba, Colombia**
5. St. Paul to Guatemala City **U.S., Mexico, Guatemala**

Page 67

Northern South America

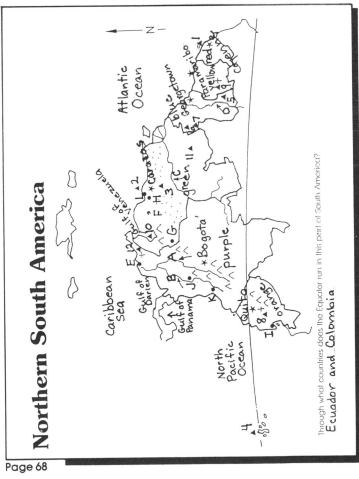

Through what countries does the Equator run in this part of South America?
Ecuador and Colombia

Page 68

Answer Key

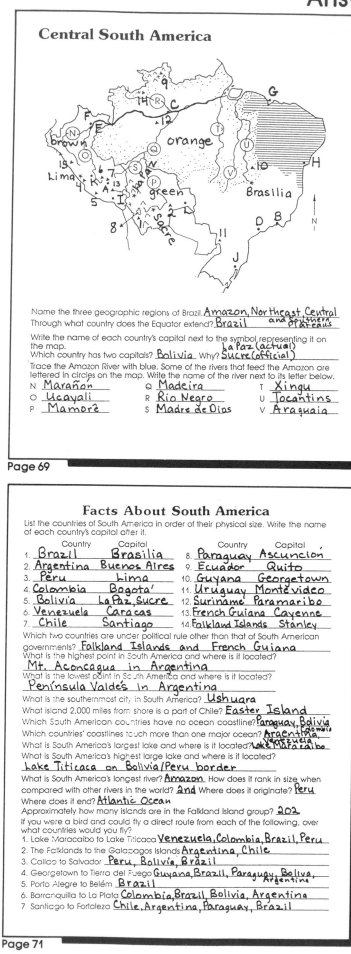

Central South America

(Page 69)

Name the three geographic regions of Brazil. **Amazon, Northeast, Central and Southern Plateaus**

Through what country does the Equator extend? **Brazil**

Write the name of each country's capital next to the symbol representing it on the map.

Which country has two capitals? **Bolivia** Why? **La Paz (actual) Sucre (official)**

Trace the Amazon River with blue. Some of the rivers that feed the Amazon are lettered in circles on the map. Write the name of the river next to its letter below.

N **Marañon**
O **Ucayali**
P **Mamoré**
Q **Madeira**
R **Rio Negro**
S **Madre de Dios**
T **Xingu**
U **Tocantins**
V **Araguaia**

Southern South America

(Page 70)

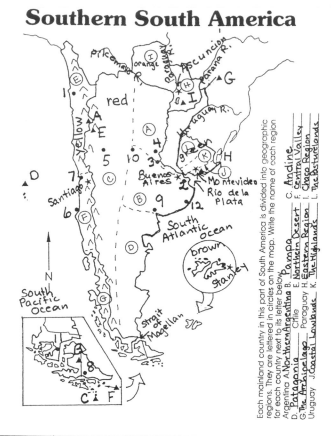

Each mainland country in this part of South America is divided into geographic regions. They are lettered in circles on the map. Write the name of each region for each country next to its letter below.

Argentina A. Northern Argentina B. Pampa C. Andine
D. Patagonia Chile E. Northern Desert F. Central Valley
G. The Archipelago Paraguay H. Eastern Region I. Chaco Region
Uruguay J. Coastal Lowlands K. The Pastorlands

Facts About South America

(Page 71)

List the countries of South America in order of their physical size. Write the name of each country's capital after it.

Country	Capital		Country	Capital
1. Brazil	Brasilia	8.	Paraguay	Ascuncion
2. Argentina	Buenos Aires	9.	Ecuador	Quito
3. Peru	Lima	10.	Guyana	Georgetown
4. Colombia	Bogotá	11.	Uruguay	Montevideo
5. Bolivia	La Paz, Sucre	12.	Suriname	Paramaribo
6. Venezuela	Caracas	13.	French Guiana	Cayenne
7. Chile	Santiago	14.	Falkland Islands	Stanley

Which two countries are under political rule other than that of South American governments? **Falkland Islands and French Guiana**

What is the highest point in South America and where is it located? **Mt. Aconcagua in Argentina**

What is the lowest point in South America and where is it located? **Península Valdés in Argentina**

What is the southernmost city in South America? **Ushuara**

What island 2,000 miles from shore is a part of Chile? **Easter Island**

Which South American countries have no ocean coastline? **Paraguay, Bolivia**

Which countries' coastlines touch more than one major ocean? **Argentina, Colombia, Venezuela**

What is South America's largest lake and where is it located? **Lake Maracaibo**

What is South America's highest large lake and where is it located? **Lake Titicaca on Bolivia/Peru border**

What is South America's longest river? **Amazon** How does it rank in size when compared with other rivers in the world? **2nd** Where does it originate? **Peru** Where does it end? **Atlantic Ocean**

Approximately how many islands are in the Falkland Island group? **202**

If you were a bird and could fly a direct route from each of the following, over what countries would you fly?

1. Lake Maracaibo to Lake Titicaca **Venezuela, Colombia, Brazil, Peru**
2. The Falklands to the Galapagos Islands **Argentina, Chile**
3. Calloo to Salvador **Peru, Bolivia, Brazil**
4. Georgetown to Tierra del Fuego **Guyana, Brazil, Paraguay, Bolivia, Argentina**
5. Porto Alegre to Belém **Brazil**
6. Barranquilla to La Plata **Colombia, Brazil, Bolivia, Argentina**
7. Santiago to Fortaleza **Chile, Argentina, Paraguay, Brazil**

The British Isles

(Page 72)

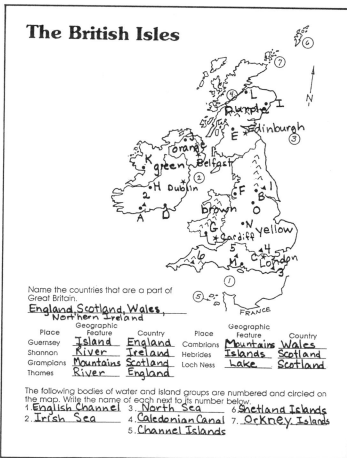

Name the countries that are a part of Great Britain.
England, Scotland, Wales, Northern Ireland

Place	Geographic Feature	Country	Place	Geographic Feature	Country
Guernsey	Island	England	Cambrians	Mountains	Wales
Shannon	River	Ireland	Hebrides	Islands	Scotland
Grampians	Mountains	Scotland	Loch Ness	Lake	Scotland
Thames	River	England			

The following bodies of water and island groups are numbered and circled on the map. Write the name of each next to its number below.

1. **English Channel**
2. **Irish Sea**
3. **North Sea**
4. **Caledonian Canal**
5. **Channel Islands**
6. **Shetland Islands**
7. **Orkney Islands**

Northern Europe

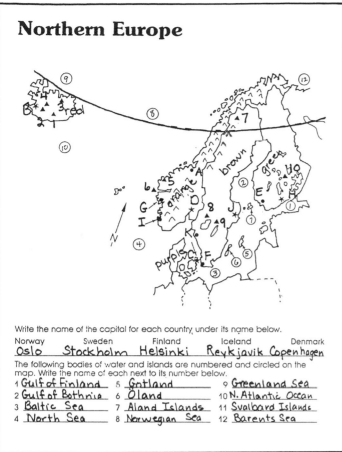

Write the name of the capital for each country under its name below.

Norway	Sweden	Finland	Iceland	Denmark
Oslo	Stockholm	Helsinki	Reykjavik	Copenhagen

The following bodies of water and islands are numbered and circled on the map. Write the name of each next to its number below.

1. Gulf of Finland
2. Gulf of Bothnia
3. Baltic Sea
4. North Sea
5. Gotland
6. Öland
7. Aland Islands
8. Norwegian Sea
9. Greenland Sea
10. N. Atlantic Ocean
11. Svalbard Islands
12. Barents Sea

France and a Neighbor

Write the name of each next to its number below.

1. Golfe de Saint-Malo
2. English Channel
3. Bay of Biscay
4. Gulf of Lion
5. Ligurian Sea
6. Mediterranean
7. Loire River
8. Seine River
9. Rhine River
10. Rhône River
11. Saône River
12. Baie de Seine
13. Dordogne River
14. Garonne River
15. Atlantic Ocean

The capital of France is Paris and of Monaco is Monaco. To whom does Corsica belong? France.

Are any of the French places' names familiar to you? ___ If yes, which ones and where do you think you may have seen their name before? _____

Answers will vary.

Netherlands, Belgium and Luxembourg

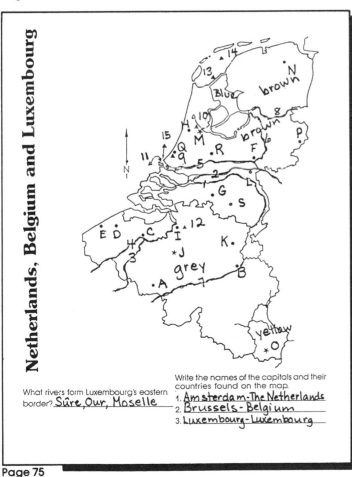

What rivers form Luxembourg's eastern border? Sûre, Our, Moselle

Write the names of the capitals and their countries found on the map.

1. Amsterdam-The Netherlands
2. Brussels-Belgium
3. Luxembourg-Luxembourg

East and West Germany

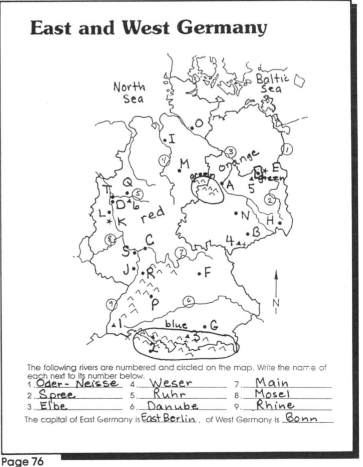

The following rivers are numbered and circled on the map. Write the name of each next to its number below.

1. Oder-Neisse
2. Spree
3. Elbe
4. Weser
5. Ruhr
6. Danube
7. Main
8. Mosel
9. Rhine

The capital of East Germany is East Berlin, of West Germany is Bonn

Answer Key

The Iberian Peninsula

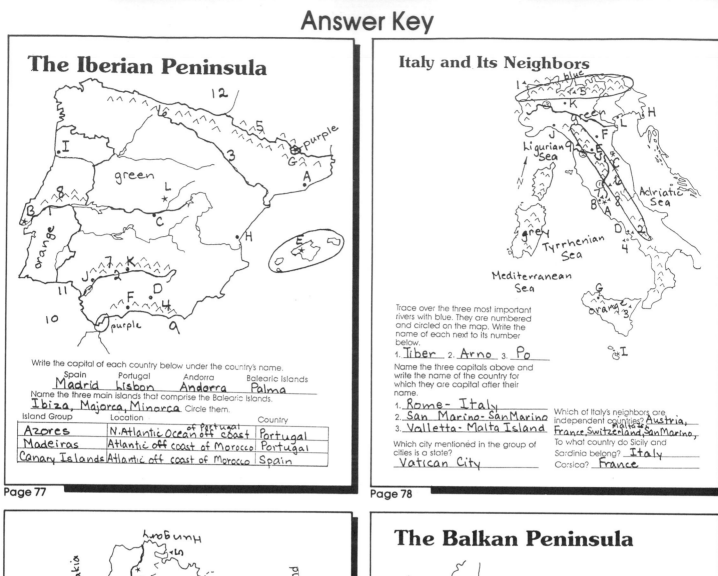

Write the capital of each country below under the country's name.

Spain	Portugal	Andorra	Balearic Islands
Madrid	Lisbon	Andorra	Palma

Name the three main islands that comprise the Balearic Islands.

Ibiza, Majorca, Minorca Circle them.

Island Group	Location	Country
Azores	N.Atlantic Ocean off coast of Portugal	Portugal
Madeiras	Atlantic off coast of Morocco	Portugal
Canary Islands	Atlantic off coast of Morocco	Spain

Italy and Its Neighbors

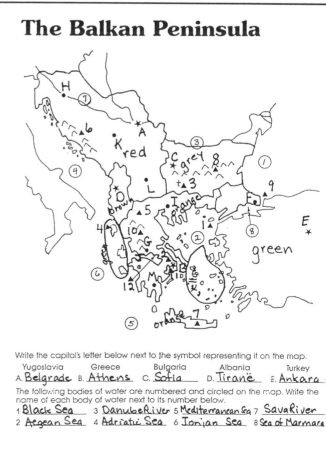

Trace over the three most important rivers with blue. They are numbered and circled on the map. Write the name of each next to its number below.

1. Tiber   2. Arno   3. Po

Name the three capitals above and write the name of the country for which they are capital after their name.

1. Rome - Italy
2. San Marino - San Marino
3. Valletta - Malta Island

Which city mentioned in the group of cities is a state?

Vatican City

Which of Italy's neighbors are independent countries? Austria, France, Switzerland, San Marino, Malta

To what country do Sicily and Sardinia belong? Italy

Corsica? France

Switzerland, Austria and Liechtenstein

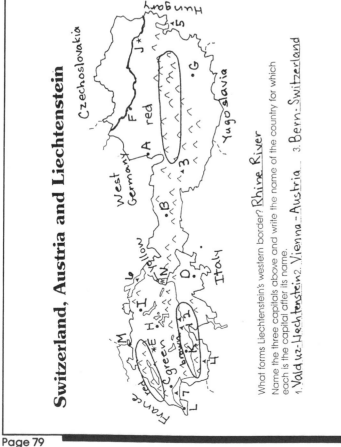

What forms Liechtenstein's western border? Rhine River

Name the three capitals above and write the name of the country for which each is the capital after its name.

1. Vaduz - Liechtenstein 2. Vienna - Austria 3. Bern - Switzerland

The Balkan Peninsula

Write the capital's letter below next to the symbol representing it on the map.

Yugoslavia	Greece	Bulgaria	Albania	Turkey
A. Belgrade	B. Athens	C. Sofia	D. Tiranë	E. Ankara

The following bodies of water are numbered and circled on the map. Write the name of each body of water next to its number below.

1 Black Sea   3 Danube River   5 Mediterranean Sea   7 Sava River
2 Aegean Sea   4 Adriatic Sea   6 Ionian Sea   8 Sea of Marmara

Answer Key

Eastern Europe

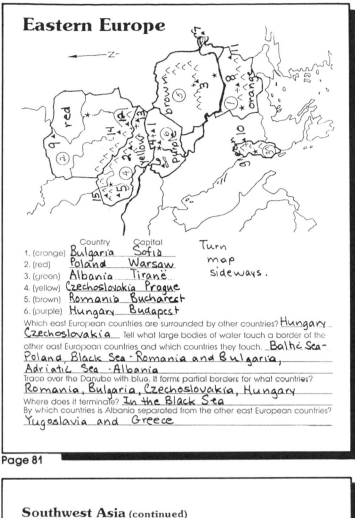

Turn map sideways.

		Country	Capital
1.	(orange)	Bulgaria	Sofia
2.	(red)	Poland	Warsaw
3.	(green)	Albania	Tiranë
4.	(yellow)	Czechoslovakia	Prague
5.	(brown)	Romania	Bucharest
6.	(purple)	Hungary	Budapest

Which east European countries are surrounded by other countries? Hungary,
Czechoslovakia Tell what large bodies of water touch a border of the
other east European countries and which countries they touch. Baltic Sea -
Poland, Black Sea - Romania and Bulgaria,
Adriatic Sea - Albania
Trace over the Danube with blue. It forms partial borders for what countries?
Romania, Bulgaria, Czechoslovakia, Hungary
Where does it terminate? In the Black Sea
By which countries is Albania separated from the other east European countries?
Yugoslavia and Greece

Page 81

Southwest Asia

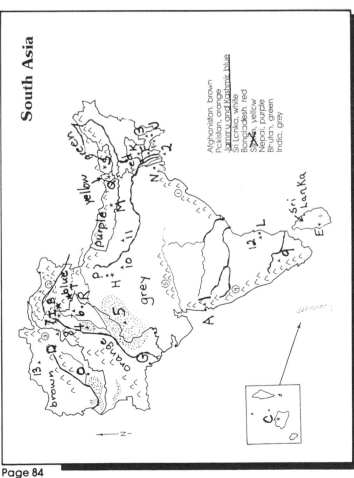

Page 82

Southwest Asia (continued)

The countries on the map are numbered and circled. Write their
names next to their numbers below. After each country's name, write the name
of its capital.

1. Turkey - Ankara
2. Syria - Damascus
3. Lebanon - Beirut
4. Israel - Jerusalem
5. Jordan - Amman
6. Iraq - Baghdad
7. Iran - Teheran
8. Kuwait - Kuwait
9. Saudi Arabia - Riyadh
10. Yemen (Sana - Sana)
11. Yemen (Aden - Aden)
12. Oman - Muscat
13. United Arab Emirates - Abu Dhabi
14. Qatar - Doha
15. Cyprus - Nicosia
16. Bahrain - Manama

Which are island countries? Cyprus, Bahrain
Which are peninsulas? Qatar, Saudi Arabia, Oman
Color the country of Oman red. What is unusual about its boundaries? A small
portion has been separated by the United Arab Emirates.
Trace over the Tigris and Euphrates Rivers with blue. Where do they start?
In Turkey
Where do they end? They empty into the Persian Gulf.
Name some ports on the Iranian side of the Persian Gulf. Bushehr,
Abadan, Bandar-e Abbas
On the Arabian side? Kuwait, Dubayy, Abu Dhabi
Doha, Dhahran, Ad Damman, Ras Tanura, Al Jubayl
What are the names of the three islands belonging to Yemen P.D.R.?
Socotra, Kamaran, Perim Circle them orange.
Label the following mountain ranges on the map.
Hejaz   Al Hajar   Anti Lebanon   Asir
Zagros   Tuwayq   Elburz
Trace over the Trans-Arabian Pipeline with green. What good is this pipeline?
It is a shortcut for transporting.

Page 83

South Asia

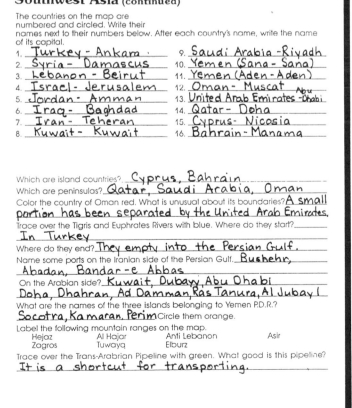

Afghanistan, brown
Pakistan, orange
Jammu and Kashmir, blue
Sri Lanka, white
Bangladesh, red
Sikkim, yellow
Nepal, purple
Bhutan, green
India, grey

Page 84

Map Skills IF8751

123

© 1990 Instructional Fair, Inc.

South Asia (continued)

Fill in the chart below. List the countries in order of their physical size. List Sikkum and Jammu and Kashmir last.

Country	Capital	Country	Capital
India	New Delhi	Sri Lanka	Colombo
Pakistan	Islamabad	Bhutan	Thimphu
Afghanistan	Kabul	Maldives	Male
Nepal	Kathmandu	Sikkim	Gangtok
Bangladesh	Dhaka	Jammu and Kashmir	Srinagar (summer) Jammu (winter)

Ganges **Bangladesh - India** Indus **Pakistan - India**
Brahmaputra **India-Bangladesh** Helmand **Afghanistan**
Krishna, Godavari and Cauvery **India**

In what countries and areas of this region are the Himalayas?
Pakistan, India, Jammu and Kashmir, Nepal, Sikkim, Bhutan

List the three highest mountains in this region, and in the world, in order. Tell where they are located. (Hint: Look in encyclopedia under "mountain.")
1. **Mt. Everest - Nepal**
2. **Mt. Godwin Austen - Pakistan**
3. **Mt. Kanchenjunga - Sikkim**

There are other mountain ranges in this region. They are numbered and circled on the map. Write their names next to their numbers below.
1. **Eastern Ghats**   3. **Hindu Kush**
2. **Karakoram Range**   4. **Western Ghats**
5. **Vindhya Range**

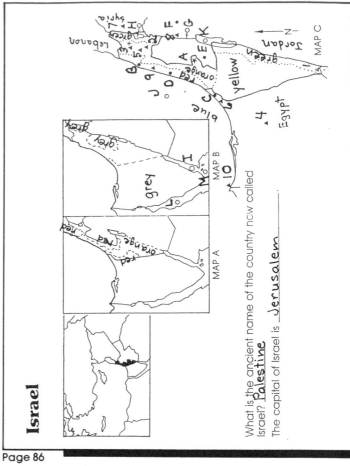

Israel

What is the ancient name of the country now called Israel? **Palestine**
The capital of Israel is **Jerusalem**

China, Mongolia and Taiwan

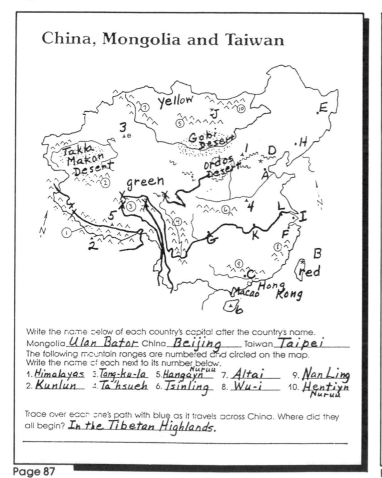

Write the name below of each country's capital after the country's name.
Mongolia **Ulan Bator** China **Beijing** Taiwan **Taipei**
The following mountain ranges are numbered and circled on the map. Write the name of each next to its number below.
1. **Himalayas** 3. **Tang-ku-la** 5. **Hangayn Nuruu** 7. **Altai** 9. **Nan Ling**
2. **Kunlun** 4. **Ta'hsueh** 6. **Tsinling** 8. **Wu-i** 10. **Hentiyn Nuruu**

Trace over each one's path with blue as it travels across China. Where did they all begin? **In the Tibetan Highlands.**

Union of Soviet Socialist Republics

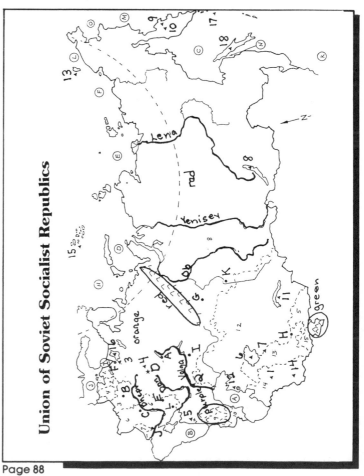

Union of Soviet Socialist Republics

The U.S.S.R. may also be called <u>Russia</u> or the <u>Soviet Union</u>.
Color the European portion orange and the Asian portion red.
What physical geographic features divide the U.S.S.R. into European and Asian sectors? <u>Caspian</u> <u>Sea and the Ural Mountains</u>.

The fifteen republics are numbered on the map. Write their number next to their name below.

9	Georgian	5	Kirghiz	
4	Lithuanian	11	Armenian	
15	Estonian	3	Byelorussian	
10	Azerbaijan	8	R.S.F.S.R.	
12	Kazakh	2	Latvian	
14	Turkmen	13	Uzbek	
6	Ukrainian	7	Moldavian	

The U.S.S.R. is the world's largest country. It spreads over a part of Europe and Asia from the <u>Baltic</u> Sea to the <u>Pacific</u> Ocean.

The capital of Russia is <u>Moscow</u>.

The following bodies of water are lettered on the map. Write their letters next to their names below.

G	Arctic Ocean	E	Laptev Sea
A	Caspian Sea	I	Gulf of Finland
H	Barents Sea	J	Baltic Sea
C	Gulf of Anadyr	B	Black Sea
E	East Siberian Sea	L	Chukchi Sea
		C	Sea of Okhotsk
		N	Tatar Strait
		K	Sea of Japan
		D	Kara Sea
		M	Bering Sea

Southeast Asia

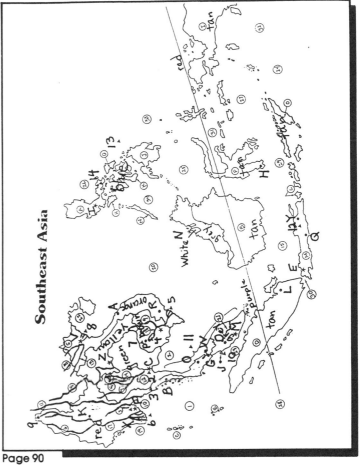

Southeast Asia (continued)

After each country's name, write the name of its capital.

Burma <u>Rangoon</u>
Laos <u>Vientiane</u>
Thailand <u>Bangkok</u>
Philippines <u>Manila</u>
Singapore <u>Singapore</u>
Brunei <u>Bandar Seri Begawan</u>
Kampuchea <u>Phnom Penh</u>
Vietnam <u>Hanoi</u>
Malaysia <u>Kuala Lumpur</u>
Indonesia <u>Jakarta</u>

Another name for Kampuchea is <u>Cambodia</u>

Trace the rivers with blue. The rivers and some other bodies of water are numbered and circled on the map. Write their numbers on the map next to their names below.

24 Timor Sea	2 Gulf of Thailand	19 Bay of Bengal	5 Lo River
31 Molucca Sea	27 Banda Sea	3 Sittang River	15 Java Sea
11 Salween River	6 Mekong River	6 Chindwin River	34 Sulu Sea
1 Andaman Sea	10 Gulf of Martaban	14 Nan River	7 Ping River
13 Black River	23 Strait of Malacca	16 Yom River	22 Gulf of Tonkin
29 Flores Sea	33 Southwest Pacific	25 Celebes Sea	17 Irrawaddy River
8 Red River	Ocean	12 Chao Phraya	32 Arafura Sea
4 Wang River	21 Pahang River	28 Indian Ocean	18 Tonle Sap River
20 China Sea	26 Philippine Sea	30 Sunda Strait	

Which countries in this region are island countries? <u>Singapore, (50)</u> <u>Indonesia, (13600)</u> <u>Philippines (7000)</u>
Find out about how many islands there are in each country and write the number after the name of the country above.

Some of the islands on the map have a circled letter on them. Write the names of those islands following their correct letters below.

A. <u>Luzon</u>	E. <u>Nicobar</u>	I. <u>New Guinea</u>	M. <u>Java</u>
B. <u>Borneo</u>	F. <u>Celebes</u>	J. <u>Mindanao</u>	N. <u>Palawan</u>
C. <u>Andaman</u>	G. <u>Samar</u>	K. <u>Negros</u>	O. <u>Timor</u>
D. <u>Sumatra</u>	H. <u>Mindoro</u>	L. <u>Bali</u>	

What two islands above actually do not belong to any of the countries of Southeast Asia? <u>Andaman and Nicobar</u>

Japan and the Koreas

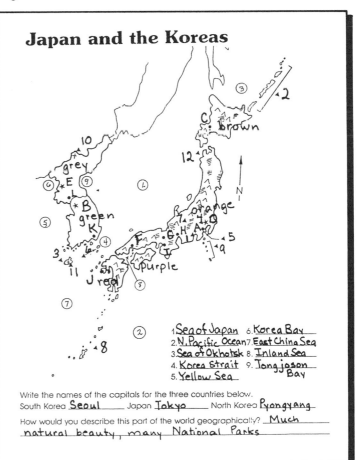

1. <u>Sea of Japan</u>   6. <u>Korea Bay</u>
2. <u>N. Pacific Ocean</u>   7. <u>East China Sea</u>
3. <u>Sea of Okhotsk</u>   8. <u>Inland Sea</u>
4. <u>Korea Strait</u>   9. <u>Tongjoson Bay</u>
5. <u>Yellow Sea</u>

Write the names of the capitals for the three countries below.
South Korea <u>Seoul</u>   Japan <u>Tokyo</u>   North Korea <u>Pyongyang</u>

How would you describe this part of the world geographically? <u>Much</u> <u>natural beauty, many National Parks</u>

Answer Key

Page 93

Facts About Eurasia

Eurasia is a name for *Europe and Asia combined.*

Several "scrambled" capitals of Europe and Asia are in the box below.
Unscramble them and write them and their numbers next to their countries.

1. LOUSE	2. KNOBGKA	3. WOMCSO	4. SBLOIN	5. TRKJAAA	6. HOINA
7. HKCOOLTMS	8. IGNEBJI	9. NARHETE	10. THASEN	11. RIEBTU	12. BADGADH
13. AAANER	14. MMATSREAD	15. ENW HILED	16. HNMPO PNHE	17. IMRDAD	
18. RAWWAS	19. NAVEIN	20. SAMDSAUC	21. SNIHLIEK	22. TUKIWA	
23. RGPAEU	24. LRBAGDEE	25. URLSEBSS	26. IETPAI	27. PNHCEENOGA	

Belgium *Brussels 25* Thailand *Bangkok 2* Indonesia *Jakarta 5*
South Korea *Seoul 1* Portugal *Lisbon 4* Russia *Moscow 3*
Denmark *Copenhagen 27* Vietnam *Hanoi 6* Kampuchea *Phnom Penh 16*
Austria *Vienna 19* Sweden *Stockholm 7* India *New Delhi 15*
Finland *Helsinki 21* Lebanon *Beirut 11* Netherlands *Amsterdam 14*
Kuwait *Kuwait 22* Syria *Damascus 20* Iraq *Baghdad 12*
Czechoslovakia *Prague 23* Iran *Teheran 9* Spain *Madrid 17*
Yugoslavia *Belgrade 24* China *Beijing 8* Poland *Warsaw 18*
Greece *Athens 10* Turkey *Ankara 13* Taiwan *Taipei 26*

Read the descriptions of several countries below. From each description write the name of the country.

This country is surrounded by Russia and China. It is *Mongolia*

This country is at the end of a peninsula in the Yellow Sea. It is *S. Korea*

This country is bordered by Spain to its southwest and by West Germany to its northeast. It is *France*

This country is on the mainland of Italy on the Adriatic Sea. It is *San Marino*

This country is bounded by the Black Sea to the east, Romania to the north, Yugoslavia to the west and by Turkey and Greece to the south. It is *Bulgaria*

This country is bordered by India to its south and west, China to the north and Sikkum to the east. It is *Nepal*

This country is an island in the Indian Ocean. It is *Sri Lanka*

The Equator runs through this country. The country is *Indonesia*

This country is physically divided by the Sea of Marmara. It is *Turkey*

This country is the largest country in the world. It is *Russia*

This country is a mountain country north and west of Italy, south of West Germany and east of France. It is *Switzerland*

Page 94

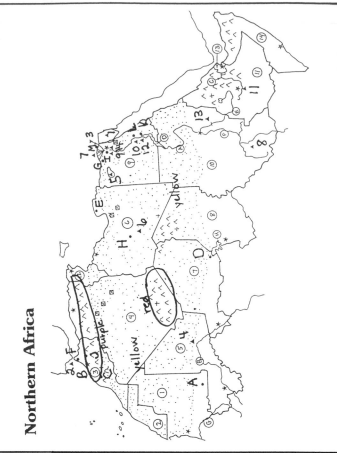

Northern Africa

Page 95

Northern Africa (continued)

The fourteen countries of Northern Africa are numbered and circled on the map. Write their number next to their name below.

2 Western Sahara 6 Libya 12 Tunisia 8 Chad 7 Niger
10 Sudan 5 Mali 9 Egypt 3 Morocco 11 Ethiopia
14 Somalia 13 Djibouti 4 Algeria 1 Mauritania

Write the number of each country next to its capital below.

9 Cairo 12 Tunis 7 Niamey 10 Khartoum
3 Rabat 5 Bamako 14 Mogadishu 11 Addis Ababa
1 Nouakchott 4 Algiers 6 Tripoli 13 Djibouti
8 N'Djamena

Circle the Atlas Mountains purple and the Ahaggar Mountains red. Color the Sahara Desert yellow. In how many countries does it reach? **12**

Which country does not have a capital? *Western Sahara*

The following bodies of water have circled letters on them on the map. Trace over or color the bodies of water with blue and write the letters on the map next to their names below.

C Awash River A The Nile G Sénégal River
E Blue Nile D Lake Nasser B Niger River
F White Nile H Lake Chad

What countries are oil producing countries? *Algeria, Libya, Egypt*
To whom do the Canary Islands belong? *Spain* Madeira Islands? *Portugal*
Name the countries and their Highest Points that are marked on the map.
Morocco - Jebel Toubkal   Algeria - Mt. Tahat
Chad - Emi Koussi   Ethiopia - Ras Dashen
Libya - Bette Peak

Page 96

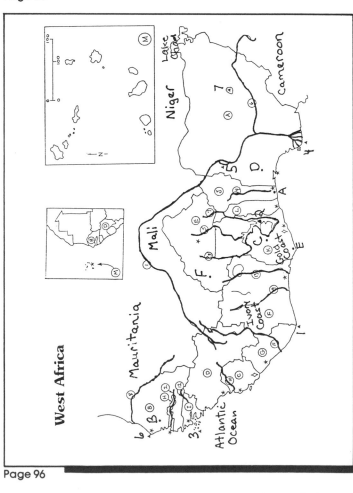

West Africa

Answer Key

West Africa (continued)

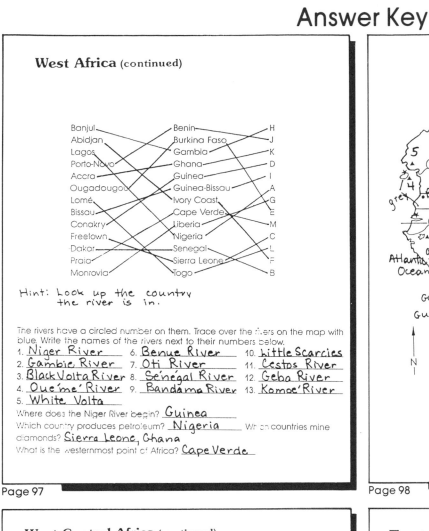

Banjul — Benin — H
Abidjan — Burkina Faso — J
Lagos — Gambia — K
Porto-Novo — Ghana — D
Accra — Guinea — I
Ougadougou — Guinea-Bissau — A
Lomé — Ivory Coast — G
Bissau — Cape Verde — E
Conakry — Liberia — M
Freetown — Nigeria — C
Dakar — Senegal — L
Praia — Sierra Leone — F
Monrovia — Togo — B

Hint: Look up the country the river is in.

The rivers have a circled number on them. Trace over the rivers on the map with blue. Write the names of the rivers next to their numbers below.

1. Niger River   6. Benue River   10. Little Scarcies
2. Gambie River   7. Oti River   11. Cestos River
3. Black Volta River 8. Sénégal River 12. Geba River
4. Oué'mé' River   9. Bandama River   13. Komoé' River
5. White Volta

Where does the Niger River begin? Guinea

Which country produces petroleum? Nigeria   Which countries mine diamonds? Sierra Leone, Ghana

What is the westernmost point of Africa? Cape Verde

West Central Africa

West Central Africa (continued)

Central African Republic (blue) Bangui
Equatorial Guinea (grey) Malabo   Congo (purple) Brazzaville
Zaire (yellow) Kinshasa   Gabon (green) Libreville
Cameroon (orange) Yaoundé'   Angola (red) Luanda
São Tomé and Príncipe (circle brown) São Tomé'

The following national parks are numbered in circles on the map. Write the number of each national park next to its name below.

6 Kundelungu   3 Mupa   6 Salonga
9 Garamba   1 Quicama   2 Cameia
4 Bikuar   7 Upemba   5 Porto Alexandre

Several rivers are marked with a circled letter. Write the name of each river next to its letter below.

A. Ubangi River   G. Benue   L. Kasai
B. Bomu   H. Ogooué'   M. Aruwimi
C. Kotto   I. Ivindo   N. Lomami
D. Lobaye   J. Canene River O. Lualaba
E. Kadei   K. Congo   P. Luvua
F. Sanaga

Where does the Congo start? In Zaire

Where does it end? South Atlantic Ocean — west side of Zaire
Name three of its tributaries. Answers will vary.

What are the names of the territories of Equatorial Guinea?
1. Fernando Po   3. Elobey Chico   5. Corsisco
2. Rio' Muni   4. Elobey Grande
Which is the mainland? Rio Muni
On which is the capital? Fernando Po

East Central Africa

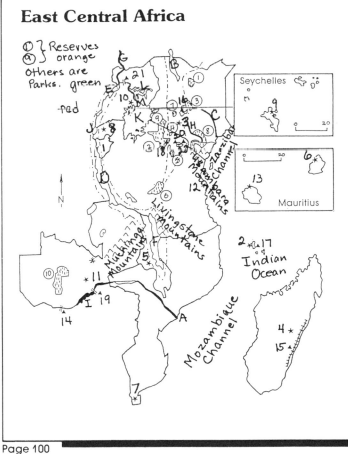

Answer Key

East Central Africa (continued)

1. Bujumbura Burundi
2. Moroni Comoros
3. Nairobi Kenya
4. Antananarivo Madagascar
5. Lilongwe Malawi
6. Port Louis Mauritius
7. Maputo Mozambique
8. Kigali Rwanda
9. Victoria Seychelles
10. Kampala Uganda
11. Lusaka Zambia
12. Dar es Salaam Tanzania
13. St. Denis Reunion

Name the island countries. Reunion, Madagascar, Seychelles, Mauritias, Comoros,

Which country is an island but under the jurisdiction of France? Reunion

Which country is on the mainland but has islands too? Tanzania

What is the mainland called? Tanganyika the islands? Zanzibar

Trace over the Equator with red. Over what countries does it extend? Uganda, Kenya

Trace the Great Rift Valley with yellow. What countries does it reach? Tanzania, Uganda, Zambia, Kenya, Rwanda, Burundi, Mozambique, Malawi

The national parks and game reserves are numbered and circled on the map. Color the national parks green and the game reserves orange. Write the name of each below next to its number.

1. Marsabit Game Reserve
2. Serengeti National Park
3. Meru National Park
4. Aberdare National Park
5. Arusha National Park
6. Tarangire National Park
7. Mt. Kenya National Park
8. Tsavo National Park
9. Masai Mara Game Reserve
10. Kafue National Park

What countries bound Lake Victoria? Kenya, Uganda, Tanzania

Where does the Zambezi River begin? Northwest Corner of Zambia

Where does it flow? Through Angola, Zambia, along the Zimbabwe border and across Mozambique

Where does it end? In the Mozambique Channel

What country is a large producer of copper? Zambia

Southern Africa

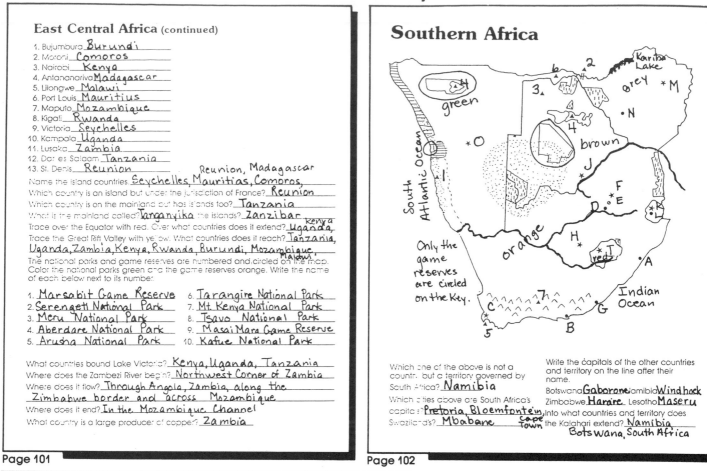

Only the game reserves are circled on the key.

Which one of the above is not a country but a territory governed by South Africa? Namibia

Which cities above are South Africa's capital? Pretoria, Bloemfontein, Cape Town

Swaziland's? Mbabane

Write the capitals of the other countries and territory on the line after their name.
Botswana Gaborone Namibia Windhoek
Zimbabwe Harare Lesotho Maseru

Into what countries and territory does the Kalahari extend? Namibia, Botswana, South Africa

About the book . . .

This book helps students increase their ability to use maps and acquire a more comprehensive understanding of the geography of the USA and the world. The activities provide in-depth experiences for students to develop their research skills. To do some of the activities, an encyclopedia or atlas will be necessary.
(You may wish to use the postal abbreviations to label the bordering states.)

About the author . . .

An experienced author and veteran teacher, with a Master's Degree in Reading and an Advanced Graduate Certificate from Washington University in Language Development, **Claire Norman** is well prepared to develop materials for children. Her 33 years of teaching experience include all of the elementary grades, remedial reading, the teaching of art, and directing the Media Center.

Author: Claire Norman
Editor: Lee Quackenbush
Editorial Assistants: Noel Bryan/Carolyn Carbery
Art/Production: Pat Biggs
Cover Art: Jan Vonk